RUBRICS

RUBRICS

A Handbook for Construction and Use

EDITED BY

Germaine L. Taggart
Fort Hays State University, Hays, KS

Sandra J. Phifer
Fort Hays State University, Hays, KS

Judy A. Nixon
Fort Hays State University, Hays, KS

Marilyn Wood
USD #489, Hays, KS

TECHNOMIC
PUBLISHING CO., INC.

LANCASTER · BASEL

Rubrics

a TECHNOMIC®  publication

Published in the Western Hemisphere by
Technomic Publishing Company, Inc.
851 New Holland Avenue, Box 3535
Lancaster, Pennsylvania 17604 U.S.A.

Distributed in the Rest of the World by
Technomic Publishing AG
Missionsstrasse 44
CH-4055 Basel, Switzerland

Printed in the United States of America
10 9 8 7 6 5 4 3 2

Main entry under title:
   Rubrics: A Handbook for Construction and Use

A Technomic Publishing Company book
Bibliography: p.
Includes index p. 149

Library of Congress Catalog Card No. 98-60082
ISBN No. 1-56676-652-4

CONTENTS

PREFACE

Rubrics: A Handbook for Construction and Use provides teachers and administrators with strategies to construct, adapt, and use rubrics. A rubric is defined as a tool for assessing instruction and performance according to predetermined expectations and criteria. The book was developed on the premise that rubrics, when used to evaluate authentic teaching and learning, are a valid and reliable assessment tool. Additionally, rubrics must be developed and used within the context of the classroom. Ownership of the rubrics is created by collaborative development and constant dialogue regarding the merits of the rubric.

Three major goals support the construction of this book. One is the development of a practical text to be used by teachers and administrators to augment the evaluation of selected performance tasks. The second is to design a document that is nonlinear in nature. Information gleaned from educators during the past two years indicates the need for a book that could assist educators in adapting existing rubrics for use in their classroom settings and to enable them to create valid and reliable instruments for assessing the performance of their students. The text provides guidance on formulating, applying, and reviewing the pros and cons of this form of alternative assessment.

A third goal is to provide assessment rubrics for administrators and teachers that will be useful in determining curriculum and performance criteria and level of accomplishment. Cross-curricular rubrics are provided, which should be useful in many classroom scenarios either as constructed or after being adapted to meet the needs of the classroom situation. The successful utilization of this book is not dependent upon use in a lock-step, sequential fashion. The user is encouraged to select desired chapters that are pertinent to the needs of the educator.

Each chapter focuses on a major aspect of rubric construction and use in classroom settings.

Chapter 1 provides a historical view of alternative assessment, rationale for using rubrics, and attempts to answer the question of how rubric use will change instructional methods. Rubrics development is linked to district and state standards.

Chapter 2 offers examples of curriculum evaluation for school improvement, showing the "why" of assessing curriculum, the way to create rubrics, and examples of staff-created rubrics.

Chapter 3 guides the reader through student implementation of rubrics. Student input into rubric development empowers students as independent learners by allowing them to select criteria for assessing their learning and by linking self-assessment and critical thinking.

Chapter 4 provides means for development of rubrics for young learners and pre-kindergarten and primary learning environments. A rationale for rubric use at pre-kindergarten and primary levels is offered with suggestions for converting rubric criteria to letter grades.

A cross-curricular approach to rubrics for assessments is provided in Chapter 5. Construction ideas and numerous examples of rubrics are provided for assessing tasks that incorporate problem solving in math and science; social studies skill; and supplemental areas such as technology, physical education, oral reports, and stories. The authors also suggest ways to convert rubrics to letter grades.

Chapter 6 discusses rubric categories and practical applications of reading and writing rubrics. Included within the chapter is a brief description of current views on the reading process, text categories, and the development of rubrics to support the process and categories. Numerous generic rubrics are provided for the reader.

Chapter 7 provides the reader with rubrics for the specialty areas of storytelling, music, and physical education. Both cognitive and affective rubrics are presented with a great deal of versatility so that the rubrics can be used for tasks in other areas as well. A discussion of criteria selection and behavior expectations highlights the section.

Two scenarios for rubric use when using the computer as an instructional tool are described in Chapter 8. The first rubric provides an analytical view of the processes of information retrieval and word processing. The second rubric looks at computer use in cooperative learning settings. Task criteria are observed in academic terms of computer use and in social skills.

Chapter 9 looks at setting meaningful criteria in rubric assessment for diverse learners. Particular emphasis is placed on language development needs and rubrics that serve to assess dependency levels.

Chapter 10 reviews rubrics as a tool for ongoing teacher evaluation, with a historical look at teacher evaluation, the linking of teaching effectiveness to teacher evaluation, and the how and why of teacher-created rubrics.

It is the sincere desire of the authors and editors that this rubric text provides an easy reference to rubric techniques and examples that fit the needs of educators in authentic school settings. Attention is focused upon portability in terms of time constraints and materials, value of rubrics that promote authentic task assessment, and ease in adaptation to support existing curricula. While the rubric samples enclosed have been proven successful in classroom settings, a word of caution must be stated. Rubrics are only as good as their ability to fit the situation for which they are used. Feel free to adapt the examples shown so that the rubrics are written at a level of understanding conducive to the learning of your students and staff. Share the rubrics prior to use with your students so that predetermined criteria are understood by all and ownership of the rubric is certain. Finally, review the rubics with all parties who have ownership in them, including parents of the students. Feel free to revise rubrics initially and in an ongoing manner as situations and criteria change, being mindful that interested parties be made aware of changes. It is only through personal adaptation and application of rubrics that fit the needs of your particular situation that rubrics can function as meaningful, objective tools for performance tasks.

ACKNOWLEDGEMENTS

We would like to acknowledge the following people for their expertise in using rubrics with students in their educational systems and for their contributions to this text:

- Julie Bliese is an experienced primary and early childhood special education teacher.
- Ethel Edwards is the Title I Coordinator with the Kansas State Department of Education and is an experienced librarian, teacher, and administrator.
- Nancy Harman is an experienced primary teacher and also has middle school experience.
- Deliece Mullen is an experienced elementary teacher and is starting a career as an elementary administrator.
- Dr. John Neal has been a high school science teacher, a technology curriculum specialist, a university professor, and is currently self-employed in the field of technology.
- Dr. Judy Nixon has been a preschool and elementary teacher and is currently an assistant professor at the university level in the College of Education.
- Dr. Sandy Phifer has been a preschool through middle school teacher and is currently an assistant professor at the university level in the College of Education.
- Dr. Craig S. Shwery has been a K–8 classroom teacher and is currently a university assistant professor at the university level in the College of Education.
- Dr. Germaine L. Taggart has been a K–9 classroom teacher and

is currently an assistant professor at the university level in the College of Education.

- Marilyn Wood is a primary classroom teacher and serves as adjunct faculty at the university level.

Special appreciation is extended to Judy Pape, Linda Garner, Brandi Clark, Patricia Duffey, and Jessi Long for their expertise in assisting the editors in producing this text.

INTRODUCTION

WHY IS THE USE OF RUBRICS IMPORTANT?

Alternative assessments are being widely discussed in educational settings as a way to evaluate both the learning process and the accountability of students. We have found that teachers want not only the background information and the link between instruction and assessment, but also the actual construction techniques for creating rubrics. Therefore, we have included many actual rubrics with explicit directions on their development. We have included several that are tools for teachers to assess students, and some in which students assess themselves or their peers. Any or all of these rubrics can be adapted to various grade or developmental levels.

As teachers, we become more attuned in judging the learning process of students as well as the product. We develop rubrics to assess all types of learners and become more effective as teachers when we see the direct link between instruction and assessment of students. We see in actuality the connection between expected and achieved success.

As students become accustomed to using rubrics to evaluate themselves, they learn criteria for achievement levels and how to set goals and strive to reach them. As they work with peers and teachers to develop these rubrics, the sense of collaboration and ownership in their learning becomes very important to them. These lessons alone build toward developing future citizens who will set goals, think critically, and work toward achieving those goals.

Readers will gain knowledge about rubric construction and use. We hope this book will benefit you in the following ways:

(1) Background information on alternative assessment

(2) The link between instruction and assessment

(3) Connections between expected and achieved success

(4) Construction techniques for creating rubrics

(5) Use of rubrics across the curriculum

(6) Examples of rubrics for all types of learners

(7) Ways for teachers to judge the learning process and accountability of students

(8) Learning becomes collaborative between the students and teacher

(9) Criteria are set for students to reach goals

Assessment That Drives Instruction

Not only do people come in all different shapes and sizes, but the ways in which they learn are also widely varied. An important realization is that all children can learn if we address the different rates and ways each learns best. Some learn best in small groups; others prefer the large group setting. Some need a hands-on approach to learning while others want to simply read about the day's lesson. Whatever the learning style, the fact remains that there is no one set way to reach all learners all of the time.

Educators have learned that the one-size-fits-all teaching theory rarely tailor-fits anyone. No longer do teachers stand at the front of the room and lecture. Today, educators work for a student-centered approach. That means classrooms are immersed with interaction, cooperation, inquiry, and challenge. The keystone of education is the student—not the teacher.

These changes in instructional delivery reflect the changes and the needs of society. During the industrial age of the early 1900s, we created a system that best met our workplace needs of assembly lines and industrial manufacturing. Schools educated students with skills to match those jobs. We graduated the best industrial-age students in the world.

As the needs of society have changed to make use of new technologies, so has the role of education changed. Students are being prepared to live, learn, and work in an international community.

The Kansas assessments were originally envisioned and created to highlight and underscore the direction for needed curriculum and instruction changes in Kansas education. The assessments grew out of, in part, the premise that what is tested is what is taught in schools. The assessments set out academic challenges and high standards for Kansas students and educators. The assessments present challenging tasks whose performance standards are expected to increase as successive performance hurdles are cleared. Further, they use unfamiliar testing methods and approaches as well as focus on content that is only now finding its way into textbooks.

The assessments grow from the Kansas Curriculum Standards in the five subject fields. Curriculum standards are targeted at higher order outcomes including critical thinking, diverse communication skills, problem solving, reasoning, and decision-making instructional outcomes. The assessments are a product of Kansas educators whose development is coordinated by the Center for Educational Testing and Evaluation at the University of Kansas.

Each year in which a content area is to be assessed, largely new testing devices are constructed for use in the different content areas. Typically, a set of questions on each examination is carried forward in order to be able to evaluate performance trends over time. The approach to development of an assessment relies almost entirely on Kansas educators and resources.

A series of steps is generally followed leading to the creation of an assessment. These steps are ordinarily as follows:

(1) The appropriate state advising committee defines the general structure and format for the assessment.

(2) Four to eight experienced, highly regarded Kansas teachers at the grade for the content area are selected based on nominations received from local districts; persons selected are trained on test development and begin the creation of the assessment questions using the applicable curriculum standards as the sole guide. Teachers work independently crafting their first draft items.

(3) The work products from the first stage are next reviewed, revised, modified, and contributed to be a second round of developers comprised of five to six Kansas curriculum specialists, administrators, and higher education subject matter specialists.

(4) The appropriate state advising committee reviews, reacts, revises, and directs changes for the emerging test questions.

(5) The appropriate advising committee begins review and alteration of the existing performance assessment scoring criteria for the content area, as well as needed revisions for the administration manuals and scoring guides.

(6) Test items surviving advisory committee review and recommendation for inclusion on the assessment are subjected to a limited field test.

(7) Items to appear on an assessment are reviewed for bias, insensitivity, and offensiveness by a committee of impacted class members; when testing is completed, empirical procedures are used to evaluate for evidence of bias.

(8) Test booklets, administration manuals, and scoring guides are finalized, printed, and distributed to districts. When results from testing identify a problem, test scoring is modified before final reports are returned to schools.

A test itself is not valid or invalid. Validity is the appropriateness of inferences made and actions taken based on test scores. The only significant and worthwhile intervention is effective teaching. Therefore, staff development must attend to instructional and curricular methods regarding how and what to teach.

Staff members must also understand the performance assessment scoring rubrics, and they must incorporate the rubric(s) into their instruction and evaluation of students. Rubrics as a term derives from "rules." The scoring rubrics offer very exacting definitions of the outcomes being evaluated. How to teach and what to focus on in the instructional process is embodied by these rubrics or rules. A careful examination of the scoring rubrics will be instructive toward helping staff know what to teach. Incorporating the rubrics as part of the local classroom pupil evaluation on projects, etc., will also inform and instruct students as to expectations. Local staff development focusing on understanding the content and substance of the rubrics will result in an understanding of what to stress and focus on during instruction.

For instance, large scale assessment in mathematics historically has required students to produce a single correct answer to a static problem. The National Council of Teachers of Mathematics (NCTM) *Curriculum and Evaluation Standards* and the *Kansas Mathematics Curriculum Standards* call for new methods of instruction, refocused curriculum efforts, and new approaches to assessment and evaluation that contain multiple correct answers and an emphasis on problem-solving skills. The Kansas Mathematics Assessment has responded to this call by incorporating open-ended questions at each of the grades tested.

There are three performance items, one each for measuring problem solving, communication, and reasoning. As a result, each item has its own rubric. For each item, instructions are to make an overall evaluation of the response. In addition, for the problem-solving item, instructors are to evaluate four steps in the problem-solving process. The four steps or components in the problem-solving process are identified as

(1) Understanding the problem
(2) Choosing a problem-solving strategy
(3) Implementing a problem-solving strategy
(4) Finding and reporting a conclusion

Each of the problem-solving components is rated independently of the others. Performance assessment does place new demands on instructors as well as new and different expectations on students. The explicit goal of performance appraisal is for teachers to evaluate how their students think and are able to solve multi-step problems. In this way, teachers can better plan and evaluate their curriculum and instruction.

The following rubrics, developed by the Kansas State Department of Education, provide general guidelines for the kinds of factors that need to be considered when evaluating the quality of a student's response (see Figures 1.1, 1.2, 1.3, and 1.4). These rubrics are considered public domain.

In reading, the explicit goal of performance appraisal is for teachers to review and evaluate how their students think and are able to grapple with and answer the comprehension questions being posed. Figure 1.5 and the text that follows detail the general rating system and scales used for evaluating students' responses to performance-based questions.

Much has been written over the years to provide guidelines for scoring students' written work. The Six-Trait Analytical Model was developed for use by teachers in district or classroom level assessment and was originally disseminated by the Northwest Educational Laboratory. There are six traits to be evaluated: ideas and content, organization, voice, word choice, sentence fluency, and conventions. Each trait, to some extent, has potential influence upon the others; and in particular, there are strong interrelationships between ideas and organization, and between voice and word choice. However, the traits are also distinct; they are to be scored separately. Thus, each paper receives six scores—one for each trait. They are not weighted, nor are they

The overall rating of a student's response to an item is to be rated on a six-point scale from zero to five, with a five (5) being the maximum rating given and a rating of zero (0) indicating no response. Specific criteria for awarding a 5, 3, or 1 rating are described below to assist in assessing and assigning a rating to the student's response. (Use ratings of 4 and 2 to further discriminate response accuracy and completeness.)

Mathematical reasoning is the ability to make selective judgments in determining one or more solutions to a given problem situation. Problems which emphasize mathematical reasoning ask students to make inferences by integrating their mathematical understandings with the data presented in the problem in order to determine one or more solutions. Mathematical reasoning includes but is not limited to geometric, proportional and spatial reasoning plus logic.

Rating of: **OVERALL RATING**

5   A **Superior** response:
         •   gives a correct response with strong, supporting arguments.
         •   uses examples and counter examples when appropriate.
         •   gives clear justification of conclusions, uses reasoning to develop correct mathematical statements.
         •   constructs valid and complete arguments.
         •   uses appropriate forms of reasoning.
         •   derives a set of logical conclusions from a set of facts.

4   Assign at your discretion to those responses falling between 5 and 3.

3   An **Adequate** response:
         •   is partially correct and has some supporting arguments.
         •   uses some inappropriate examples or counter examples.
         •   gives a somewhat clear justification of conclusions.
         •   uses partially correct reasoning to develop partially correct mathematical statements.
         •   constructs partially valid or partially complete arguments.
         •   uses somewhat appropriate forms of mathematical reasoning.
         •   derives somewhat partially logical conclusions from a set of facts.

2   Assign at your discretion to those responses falling between 3 and 1.

1   An **Inadequate** response:
         •   is incorrect with little or no supporting argument.
         •   uses inappropriate examples or counter examples or no examples given.
         •   gives unclear justification of incorrect conclusions.
         •   uses incorrect reasoning to develop incorrect conclusions.
         •   constructs invalid or incomplete arguments.
         •   uses inappropriate forms of mathematical reasoning.
         •   derives illogical conclusions from a set of facts.

0   **No response:**
         •   The question was left blank.
         •   no attempt was made to respond to the problem.
         •   no information was given to allow any judgment.

Figure 1.1 *Overall Rating Scoring Rubric for Mathematical Reasoning.*

The overall rating of a student's response to an item is to be rated on a six-point scale from zero to five, with a five (5) being the maximum rating given and a rating of zero (0) indicating no response. Specific criteria for awarding a 5, 3, or 1 rating are described below to assist in assessing and assigning a rating to the student's response. (Use ratings of 4 and 2 to further discriminate response accuracy and completeness.)

Communicating mathematics means mathematical vocabulary, language, notations, and symbols are used to describe or interpret mathematical concepts, procedures, and relationships. Problems which emphasize mathematical communication ask students to interpret or create mathematical ideas in a variety of written, oral or visual formats.

Rating of: **OVERALL RATING**

5   A **Superior** response:
- responds to all aspects of the problem, is clear and unambiguous in the presentation of ideas.
- presents data accurately.
- uses appropriate mathematical vocabulary, notation and symbolism.
- includes examples, diagrams, models or graphs when appropriate.
- explains the mathematical concepts and procedures used.
- interprets and/or communicates a solution in terms of the data defined in the problem.
- provides accurate, clear and precise response.
- organizes and records data in an orderly manner if appropriate.

4   Assign at your discretion to those responses falling between 5 and 3.

3   An **Adequate** response:
- responds to some aspects of the problem.
- is somewhat unclear and ambiguous in the presentation of ideas.
- presents some data accurately.
- uses both appropriate and inappropriate mathematical vocabulary, notations and symbolism.
- explains some of the mathematical concepts and procedures used.
- interprets and/or communicates a partial solution in terms of the data defined in the problem.
- responds somewhat accurately and clear.

2   Assign at your discretion to those responses falling between 3 and 1.

1   An **Inadequate** response:
- is not complete in responding to any aspect of the problem.
- is unclear or confusing in the presentation of ideas.
- uses inappropriate mathematical vocabulary, notation, or symbolism.
- interprets or communicates a solution without using data from the problem.
- contains words, examples or diagrams that do not reflect the problem.
- is not accurate or clear.

0   **No response:**
- The question was left blank.
- no attempt was made to respond to the problem.
- no information was given to allow any judgment.

Figure 1.2 Overall Rating Scoring Rubric for Communication.

6

The OVERALL rating of a student's response to an item is to be rated on a six-point scale from zero to five, with a five (5) being the maximum rating given and a rating of zero (0) indicating no response. Specific criteria for awarding a 5, 3, or 1 rating are described below to assist in assessing and assigning a rating to the student's response. (Use ratings of 4 and 2 to further discriminate response accuracy and completeness.)

Rating of: **OVERALL RATING**

5   A **Superior** response:
        • is complete in responding to all aspects of the question.
        • is clear and unambiguous.
        • communicates effectively.
        • shows mathematical understanding of the problem's ideas and requirements.
        • offers a unique explanation or representation of the problem.
        • includes examples of diagrams when appropriate.
        • focuses on all the important elements of the problem.
        • shows strong reasoning.
        • includes only minor computational errors, if any.

4   Assign at your discretion to those responses falling between 5 and 3.

3   An **Adequate** response:
        • is not totally complete in responding to all aspects of the problem.
        • shows some deficiencies in understanding aspects of the problem.
        • is somewhat confusing or unclear in the presentation of ideas.
        • indicates some understanding of required mathematical ideas, but misconceptions are evident.
        • may present information that is only partially correct.
        • exhibits incomplete reasoning.
        • omits parts or elements of the problems.
        • includes examples or diagrams that are unclear or inappropriate.
        • contains computation errors, either major or minor.

2   Assign at your discretion to those responses falling between 3 and 1.

1   An **Inadequate** response:
        • attempts, but fails to answer or complete the question.
        • shows very limited or no understanding of the problem.
        • contains major computational errors.
        • focuses entirely on the wrong mathematical idea or procedure.
        • includes explanations or reasoning that are not understandable.
        • shows copied parts of the problem with no attempt at a solution.
        • contains words, examples, or diagrams that do not reflect the problem.

0   **No response:**
        • The question was left blank.
        • no attempt was made to respond to the problem.
        • no information was given to allow any judgment.

Figure 1.3 Overall Rating Scoring Rubric for Problem Solving.

Each problem-solving process component is to be rated on a six-point scale, with a five (5) being the maximum rating given and a rating of zero (0) indicating no response. Specific criteria for awarding a 5, 3 or 1 are described for each of the process components to assist in assessing and assigning a rating to the student's response. (Use ratings of 4 and 2 to further discriminate the adequacy of a response.)

Understanding the Problem

The first step in the problem-solving process is to correctly identify the problem. In general, you are trying to determine if the student's response demonstrates that the problem/question asked is correctly understood. More specifically, ask yourself if the student's response:

- recognizes what is being asked.
- identifies what information is known and what information is missing.
- demonstrates an understanding and knowledge of the mathematical language used in the problem.
- summarizes, paraphrases, or uses diagrams to clarify the problem.
- identifies additional conditions or restrictions not given in the original problem statement.

In scoring this component, assign a rating from 0 to 5 based on the following:

Rating of:

5 The response demonstrates a complete understanding of the problem.
4 Assign at your discretion to those responses falling between 5 and 3.
3 The response demonstrates that part of the problem is misunderstood or misinterpreted.
2 Assign at your discretion to those responses falling between 3 and 1.
1 The response demonstrates a complete misunderstanding of the problem.
0 No response is given.

Choosing a Problem-Solving Strategy

The second step in the problem-solving process is to explore, identify and choose a problem-solving strategy for solving the problem identified by the student. Remember, there may be more than one strategy. In general, you are trying to determine if the student's response demonstrates an awareness, recognition and selection of an appropriate problem-solving strategy which may be used to solve the problem. More specifically ask yourself if the student's response:

- identifies a series of steps needed to solve the problem.
- identifies one or more sub-problems needed to determine the final solution.
- identifies and organizes appropriate data to assist in solving the problem.
- chooses one or more appropriate problem-solving strategies.
- uses diagrams, charts, or phrases to clarify the problem-solving strategy.
- identifies available technology or manipulatives which can be used to assist in solving the problem.

In scoring this component, assign a rating from 0 to 5 based on the following.

Rating of:

5 The response demonstrates at least one appropriate problem-solving strategy chosen to solve the problem identified by the student.
4 Assign at your discretion to those responses falling between 5 and 3.
3 The response demonstrates a partially correct problem-solving strategy was chosen to solve the problem identified by the student.
2 Assign at your discretion to those responses falling between 3 and 1.
1 The response demonstrates an incorrect problem-solving strategy was chosen to solve the problem identified by the student.
0 No response is given.

Figure 1.4 *Problem-Solving Process Components Scoring Rubric.*

8

Specific criteria for awarding a 5, 3 or 1 are described for each of the process components to assist in assessing and assigning a rating to the student's response. (Use ratings of 4 and 2 to further discriminate the adequacy of a response.)

Implementing a Problem-Solving Strategy

The third step in the problem-solving process is to implement correctly the problem-solving strategy chosen. In general, you are trying to determine if the student's response reveals accurate and consistent use of appropriate mathematical concepts and procedures to implement the problem-solving strategy chosen by the student. More specifically ask yourself if the student's response:

- shows correct implementation of the problem-solving strategy chosen by the student.
- uses sequential steps to implement the problem-solving strategy chosen by the student.
- performs required computations accurately.
- uses available technology or manipulatives correctly.

In scoring this component, assign a rating from 0 to 5 based on the following:

Rating of:

5   The response demonstrates an accurate implementation of the problem-solving strategy chosen by the student.
4   Assign at your discretion to those responses falling between 5 and 3.
3   The response demonstrates a problem-solving strategy chosen by the student that is implemented correctly, but contains copying errors, computational errors, or a partial solution.
2   Assign at your discretion to those responses falling between 3 and 1.
1   The response demonstrates an inaccurate implementation of the problem-solving strategy chosen by the student.
0   No response is given.

Finding and Reporting a Conclusion

The final step in the problem-solving process is to find and report a solution from the problem-solving strategy used. In general, you are trying to determine if the student's response clearly and correctly identifies a reasonable solution to the problem identified by the student. More specifically ask yourself if the student's response:

- presents a solution which is reasonable and plausible to the problem identified by the student.
- includes checking or verification of the solution.
- identifies and correctly labels answers.
- shows evidence of reinvestigating a problem-solving strategy if the original solution is not reasonable.
- interprets and/or communicates the solution in terms of the data used in the problem.

In scoring this component, assign a rating from 0 to 5 based on the

Rating of:

5   The response demonstrates an accurate finding and reporting of a solution to the problem identified by the student.
4   Assign at your discretion to those responses falling between 5 and 3.
3   The response demonstrates a partially accurate finding and reporting of the solution to the problem identified by the student.
2   Assign at your discretion to those responses falling between 3 and 1.
1   The response demonstrates an in-accurate finding and reporting of the solution to the problem identified by the student.
0   No response is given.

Figure 1.4 (continued) *Problem-Solving Process Components Scoring Rubric.*

9

Rating of:	Scale Description
5	The written answer demonstrates a thorough understanding of the text related to the question. It includes all of the significant and accurate textual information needed for a complete answer to the question. The answer shows evidence of the student choosing the appropriate information source to answer the question. The sources include: • information from one sentence in the text. • combined information from different sentences in the text and make the connections in the written answer. • use of reader's knowledge and the text.
4	The written answer demonstrates an essential understanding of the text related to the question. It includes most of the significant and accurate textual information needed for a complete answer to the question. There may be some minor details, but no inaccuracies. The answer shows evidence of the student choosing the appropriate information source to answer the question. The sources include: • information from one sentence to the next. • combined information from different sentences in the text and make the connections in the written answer. • use of reader's knowledge and the text.
3	The written answer demonstrates a limited understanding of the text related to the question. It includes some of the significant and accurate textual information, but may include some minor details and inaccuracies also. The answer shows evidence of the student choosing the appropriate information source to answer the question. The sources include: • information from one sentence to the next. • combined information from different sentences in the text and make the connections in the written answer. • use of reader's knowledge and the text.
2	The written answer demonstrates little understanding of the text related to the question. The answer includes little significant and accurate textual information and some minor details and inaccuracies. The minor details and inaccuracies dominate the answer. • information from one sentence in the text. • combined information from different sentences in the text and make the connections in the written answer. • use of reader's knowledge and the text.
1	The written answer demonstrates no understanding of the text related to the question. The answer includes no significant and accurate textual information related to the question. It may include textual information which is irrelevant to the question. The minor details and inaccuracies dominate the answer. It may include nontextual information related to the question. The answer may not use any information sources from the text. It may use the reader's knowledge based on non-textual information.
0	No Response. The question is left blank.
Note:	Accurate and relevant information that is added from the reader's prior knowledge is acceptable. It neither adds nor detracts from the rating to be given.

* This scoring rubric and the other detailed scoring guides were developed by the Kansas State Department of Education.

Figure 1.5 General Scoring Rubric.

summed or averaged in any way. Averaging undermines the intention of the model, which is to show that writing can be very strong in one or more areas, yet weaker in other areas.

Figure 1.6 provides a visual display of the Six-Trait Analytical Model. In addition, a detailed presentation defining the scoring of each trait follows the illustration.

In science, the explicit goal of performance appraisal is for teachers to review and evaluate how their students think and solve multi-step

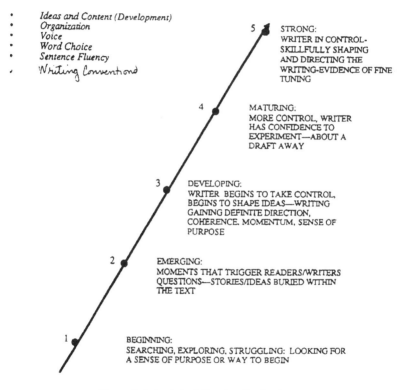

- *Ideas and Content (Development)*
- *Organization*
- *Voice*
- *Word Choice*
- *Sentence Fluency*
- *Writing Conventions*

5 STRONG:
WRITER IN CONTROL-
SKILLFULLY SHAPING
AND DIRECTING THE
WRITING-EVIDENCE OF FINE
TUNING

4 MATURING:
MORE CONTROL, WRITER
HAS CONFIDENCE TO
EXPERIMENT—ABOUT A
DRAFT AWAY

3 DEVELOPING:
WRITER BEGINS TO TAKE CONTROL,
BEGINS TO SHAPE IDEAS—WRITING
GAINING DEFINITE DIRECTION,
COHERENCE. MOMENTUM, SENSE OF
PURPOSE

2 EMERGING:
MOMENTS THAT TRIGGER READERS/WRITERS
QUESTIONS—STORIES/IDEAS BURIED WITHIN
THE TEXT

1 BEGINNING:
SEARCHING, EXPLORING. STRUGGLING: LOOKING FOR
A SENSE OF PURPOSE OR WAY TO BEGIN

Figure 1.6 *Analytical Scoring Guide: Traits.*

TRAIT: IDEAS AND CONTENT
(Development)

Rating of 5 (Strong): This paper is clear, focused, and interesting. It holds the reader's attention. Relevant anecdotes and details enrich the central theme or storyline. Ideas are fresh and original.

* The writer seems to be writing from experiences and shows insight; a good sense of how events unfold, how people respond to life and to each other.
* Supporting, relevant, telling details give the reader important information that he or she could not personally bring to the text.
* The writing has balance: main ideas stand out.
* The writer seems in control and develops the topic in an enlightening, entertaining way.
* The writer works with and shapes ideas, making connections and sharing insights.

Rating of 3 (Developing): The paper is clear and focused. The topic shows promise, even though development is still limited, sketchy or general.

* The writer is beginning to define the topic, but is not there yet. It is pretty easy to see where the writer is headed, though more information is needed to "fill in the blanks."
* The writer does seem to be writing from experience, but has some trouble going from general observations to specifics.
* Ideas are reasonably clear and purposeful, even though they may not be explicit, detailed, personalized, or expanded to show a depth of understanding.
* Support is attempted, but doesn't go far enough yet in expanding, clarifying, or adding new insights.
* Themes or main points seem a blend of the original and the predictable.

Rating of 1 (Beginning): As yet, the paper has no clear sense of purpose or central theme. To extract meaning from the text, the reader must make inferences based on sketchy details. More than one of the following problems is likely to be evident:

* Information is very limited or unclear.
* The text is very repetitious, or reads like a collection of random thoughts from which no central theme emerges.
* Everything seems as important as everything else; the reader has a hard time sifting out what's critical.
* The writer has not yet begun to define the topic in a meaningful or personal way.
* The writer may still be in search of a real topic, or sense of direction to guide development.

TRAIT: ORGANIZATION

Rating of 5 (Strong): The organization enhances and show-cases the central idea or theme. The order, structure, or presentations are compelling and moves the reader through the text.

* Details seem to fit where they're placed; sequencing is logical and effective.
* An inviting introduction draws the reader in; a satisfying conclusion leaves the reader with a sense of resolution.
* Pacing is very well controlled; the writer delivers needed information at just the right moment, then moves on.
* Transitions are smooth and weave the separate threads of meaning into one cohesive whole.
* Organization flows so smoothly the reader hardly thinks about it.

Rating of 3 (Developing): The organizational structure is strong enough to move the reader from point to point without undue confusion.

* The paper has a recognizable introduction and conclusion. The introduction may not create a strong sense of anticipation; the conclusion may not leave the reader with a satisfying sense of resolution.
* Sequencing is usually logical. It may sometimes be too obvious, or otherwise ineffective.
* Pacing is fairly well controlled, though the writer sometimes spurts ahead too quickly or spends too much time on the obvious.
* Transitions often work well; at times though, connections between ideas are fuzzy or call for inferences.
* Despite a few problems, the organization does not seriously get in the way of the main point or story-line.

Rating of 1 (Beginning): The writing lacks a clear sense of direction. Ideas, details or events seem strung together in a random, haphazard fashion--or else there is no identifiable internal structure at all. More than one of the following problems is likely to be evident:

* The writer has not yet drafted a real lead or conclusion.
* Transitions are not yet clearly defined; connections between ideas seem confusing or incomplete.
* Sequencing, if it exists, needs work.
* Pacing feels awkward, with lots of time spent on minor details or big, hard-to-follow leaps from point to point.
* Lack of organization makes it hard for the reader to get a grip on the main point or story-line.

Figure 1.6 (continued) Analytical Scoring Guide: Traits.

TRAIT: VOICE

Rating of 5 (Strong): The writer speaks directly to the reader in a way that is individualistic, expressive, and engaging. Clearly, the writer is involved in the text and is writing to be read.

- The paper is honest and written from the heart; it has the ring of conviction.
- The language is natural yet provocative; it brings the topic to life.
- The reader feels a strong sense of interaction with the writer and senses the person behind the words.
- The projected tone and voice give flavor to the writer's message and seem very appropriate for the purpose and audience.

Rating of 3 (Developing): The writer seems sincere, but not genuinely engaged, committed, or involved. The result is pleasant and sometimes even personable, but short of compelling.

- The writing communicates in an earnest, pleasing manner. Moments here and there amuse, surprise, delight or move the reader.
- Voice may emerge strongly on occasion, then retreat behind general, vague, tentative, or abstract language.
- The writing hides as much of the writer as it reveals.
- The writer seems aware of an audience, but often fails to weigh words carefully, or strands at a distance and avoids risk.

Rating of 1 (Beginning): The writer seems indifferent, uninvolved or distanced from the topic and/or the audience. As a result, the writing is flat, lifeless or mechanical; depending on the topic, it may be overly technical or jargonistic. More than one of the following problems is likely to be evident:

- The reader has a had time sensing the writer behind the words. The writer does not seem to reach out to an audience, or make use of voice to connect with that audience.
- The writer speaks in a kind of monotone that tends to flatten all potential high's and low's of the message.
- The writing communicates on a functional level, with no apparent attempt to move or involve the reader.
- The writer is not yet sufficiently engaged or at home with the topic to take risks or share her himself.

TRAIT: WORD CHOICE

Rating of 5 (Strong): Words convey the intended message in an interesting, precise, and natural way. The wording is full and rich, yet concise.

- Words are specific and accurate; they seem just right.
- Imagery is strong.
- Powerful verbs give the writing energy.
- Striking words and phrases often catch the reader's eye, but the language is natural and never overdone.
- Expression is fresh and appealing; slang is used sparingly.

Rating of 3 (Developing): The language is functional, even if it lacks punch; it does get the message across.

- Words are almost always correct and adequate (though not necessarily precise); it is easy to understand what the writer means.
- Familiar words and phrases communicate, but rarely capture the reader's imagination. The writer seems reluctant to stretch.
- the writer usually avoids experimenting; however, the paper may have one or two fine moments.
- Attempts at colorful language often come close to the mark, but may seem overdone or out of place.
- A few energetic verbs liven things up now and then; the reader yearns for more.
- The writer may lean a little on redundancy, or slip in cliché--but never relies on these crutches to the point of annoyance.

Rating of 1 (Beginning): The writer struggles with a limited vocabulary, searching for words to convey meaning. More than one of the following problems is likely to be evident:

- Language is so vague and abstract (e.g., *It was a fun time, it was nice and stuff*) that only the most general message comes through.
- Persistent redundancy clouds the message and distracts the reader.
- Clichés or jargon serve as a crutch.
- Words are used incorrectly in more than one or two cases, sometimes making the message hard to decipher.
- The writer is not yet selecting words that would help the reader to have a better understanding.
- structure, or presentation is compelling and moves the reader through the text.
- Details seem to fit where they're placed; sequencing is logical and effective.

Figure 1.6 (continued) Analytical Scoring Guide: Traits.

TRAIT: SENTENCE FLUENCY

Rating of 5 (Strong): The writing has an easy flow and rhythm when read aloud. Sentences are well built, with consistently strong and varied structure that makes expressive oral reading easy and enjoyable.

* Sentence structure reflects logic and sense, helping to show how ideas relate. Purposeful sentence beginnings guide the reader readily from one sentence to another.
* The writing sounds natural and fluent; it glides along with one sentence flowing effortlessly into the next.
* Sentences display an effective combination of power and grace.
* Variation in sentence structure and length adds interest to the text.
* Fragments, if used at all, work well.
* Dialogue, if used, sounds natural.

Rating of 3 (Developing): The text hums along efficiently for the most part, though it may lack a certain rhythm or grace. It tends to be more pleasant or businesslike than musical, more mechanical than fluid.

* The writer shows good control over simple sentence structure, more variable control over complex sentence structure.
* Sentences may not seem skillfully crafted or musical, but they are grammatical and solid. They hang together. They get the job done.
* The writer may tend to favor a particular pattern (e.g., subject-verb), but there is at least some variation in sentence length and structure (sentence beginnings are NOT all alike).
* The reader sometimes has to hunt for clues (e.g., connecting words like *however, therefore, naturally, on the other hand, to be specific, for example, next, first of all, later, still,* etc.) that show how one sentence leads into the next.
* Some parts of the text invite expressive oral reading; others may be a little stiff, choppy or awkward. Overall, it's pretty easy to read this paper aloud if you practice.

Rating of 1 (Beginning): The paper is difficult to follow or read aloud. Most sentences tend to be choppy, incomplete, rambling, or awkward; they need work. More than one of the following problems is likely to be evident:

* Sentences do not sound natural, the way someone might speak. Word patterns are often jarring or irregular, forcing the reader to pause or read over.
* Sentence structure tends to obscure meaning, rather than showing the reader how ideas relate.
* word patterns are very monotonous (e.g., subject-verb, subject-verb-object). There is little or no real variety in length or structure.
* Sentences may be very choppy. Or, words may run together in one giant "sentence" linked by *"and's"* or other connectives.
* The text does not invite expressive oral reading.

TRAIT: WRITING CONVENTIONS

Rating of 5 (Strong): The writer demonstrates a good grasp of standard writing conventions (e.g., grammar, capitalization, punctuation, usage, spelling, paragraphing) and uses them effectively to enhance readability. Errors tend to be so few and minor the reader can easily skim right over them unless specifically searching for them.

* Paragraphing tends to be sound and to reinforce the organizational structure.
* Grammar and usage are correct and contribute to clarity and style.
* Punctuation is smooth and guides the reader through the text.
* Spelling is generally correct, even on more difficult words.
* The writer may manipulate conventions-- particularly grammar--for stylistic effect.
* The writing is sufficiently long and complex to allow the writer to show skill in using a wide range of conventions (This criterion applies to grade 7 & up only.)
* Only light editing would be required to polish the text for publication.

Rating of 3 (Developing): The writer shows reasonable control over a limited range of standard writing conventions. However, the paper would require moderate editing prior to publication. Errors are numerous or serious enough to be somewhat distracting, but the writer handles some conventions well.

* Spelling is usually correct (or reasonably phonetic) on common words.
* Terminal (end-of-sentence) punctuation is almost always correct; internal punctuation (commas, apostrophes, semicolons) may be incorrect or missing.
* Problems with grammar usage are not serious enough to distort meaning.
* Paragraphing is attempted. Paragraphs sometimes run together or begin in the wrong places.
* The paper seems to reflect light, but not extensive or thorough, editing.

Rating of 1 (Beginning): Errors in spelling, punctuation, usage and grammar, capitalization and/or paragraphing repeatedly distract the reader and make the text difficult to read. More than one of the following problems is likely to be evident:

* The reader must read once to decode, then again for meaning.
* Spelling errors are frequent, even on common words.
* Punctuation (including terminal punctuation) is often missing or incorrect.
* Paragraphing is missing, irregular, or so frequent (e.g., every sentence) that it does not relate to organization of the text.
* Errors in grammar and usage are very noticeable, and may affect meaning.
* Extensive editing would be required to polish the text for publication.

Figure 1.6 (continued) Analytical Scoring Guide: Traits.

problems. Figure 1.7 is the presentation of a scoring rubric for making an overall rating to all projects. Scoring rubrics for teachers and students are then presented for the different grade levels (see Figures 1.8, 1.9, and 1.10).

Historically, large-scale assessment in social studies has required students to produce a single correct answer to a static problem. The *Kansas Curricular Standards for Social Studies* calls for new methods of instruction, refocused curriculum efforts, and new approaches to assessment and evaluation that contain an emphasis on student-

— ALL GRADES —

This overall scoring rubric provides general guidelines to the kinds of factors that need to be considered when evaluating the quality of a student's response to a specific problem. However, in the end the actual rating assigned a response will rely heavily on the <u>expert judgment</u> and overall impression of the person making the rating. There will be <u>no</u> clear-cut correct/incorrect responses to most of the problems. Rather, there will be degrees of appropriateness based on the quality of the total response in relation to what was requested by a specific problem. This rubric should be used for the overall score at all grade levels and for all projects and questions.

The **OVERALL** rating of a student's response to an item is to be placed on a six-point scale from zero to five, with a five (5) being the maximum rating given and a rating of zero (0) indicating no response. Specific criteria for awarding a 5, 3, 1 or 0 rating are described below to assist in assessing and assigning an overall rating to the student's response. (Use ratings of 4 and 2 to further discriminate response accuracy and completeness.) The overall rating is <u>not</u> simply a sum or average of the process ratings. The overall rating addresses the <u>completeness and accuracy</u> of the total response.

OVERALL SCORING RUBRIC VALUES

0	1	-2-	3	-4-	5
• No response was made • No information was given that allows for evaluation of the concepts and ideas being addressed in the problem. • Refusal to respond.	• Responses show little or no understanding of the concepts and ideas addressed. • Misconceptions are evident. • Communications poor with no rationale given for decisions, conclusions, etc. • Very little appropriate data is collected. • Conclusions, if given, are not supported by data.		• Responses lack clarity, but show some understanding of the scientific concepts and ideas addressed. • Tools are used to gather, record, and organize appropriate data, but the record is not complete. • Display of information is generally clear. • Communication is ambiguous in parts and clear in others. • Supports most conclusions with evidence. • Does not mention need for additional data when appropriate. • May mention application to real life. • Some major error is found.		• Responses are clear and show an in-depth understanding of the scientific concepts and ideas addressed. • Processes and tools are used to gather, record and organize appropriate data in logical fashion. • When information is presented in graphs, tables, etc., display is clear and includes labels. • Communication is clear, effective and unambiguous. • Writes strong, supporting conclusions. • Notes the need for additional data when appropriate. • Makes connections to real life application. • No major errors are found at this level though some minor flaws are permissible.

Figure 1.7 Science Overall Scoring Rubric.

Evaluation Guidelines for Process Components

The following matrix specifies the general evaluation criteria for the process component ratings which could be applied to various performance assessments (e.g., projects, experiments, restricted responses) at Grade 5. Use it as a general reference throughout scoring.

Scoring Manual Rubric
Grade 5

	5	3	1[*]
Recognizes and Defines Problem	☐ Observes and describes the materials and includes comparisons of how they are alike and different.	☐ Describes the materials by telling only what can be seen.	☐ Lists some materials but it is not clear what has been observed.
	☐ Writes a question related to the problem that can be tested.	☐ Writes a question that can be tested but does not relate to the problem.	☐ Writes a question but it cannot be tested. or writes a prediction that something will happen.
Designs Problem/ Solving Strategy	☐ Writes a plan that has a descriptive list of materials and specific steps that can be followed.	☐ Writes a plan that gives some materials and some steps to be followed.	☐ Lists some materials or describes a part of the experiment.
	☐ Describes an appropriate method(s) for making observations or taking measurements that will help answer question.	☐ Partially describes how to make observations or take measurements.	☐ Describes an activity where data collection is possible without saying how observations or measurements will be made.
Implements Problem/ Solving Strategy	☐ Follows plan completely.	☐ Partially follows plan.	☐ Does not follow plan very well.
	☐ Organizes and records information using charts, tables, graphs and/or pictures and labels them correctly.	☐ Organizes information which only represents part of the data collected or if complete, has labels missing.	☐ Writes down some numbers or observations without organizing them.
Interprets and Communicates Findings and Conclusions	☐ Compares the observations and measurements from testing and gives a conclusion based upon this information.	☐ Gives a conclusion based upon only part of the information collected.	☐ Retells information.
	☐ Answers original question.	☐ Answers a question related to the problem, but it is not original question.	☐ Writes about ideas related to the experiment but does not answer a question of study.
	☐ Explains why conclusion was reached and its importance.	☐ Retells part(s) of the experiment to explain something done or learned.	☐ Does not write about the importance and meaning of conclusion. Tells why the project was fun.

[*] Use the rating of "0" to indicate that no response was given.

Figure 1.8.

Evaluation Guidelines for Process Components

The following matrix specifies the general evaluation criteria for the process component ratings which could be applied to various performance assessments (e.g. projects, experiments, restricted responses) at Grade 8. Use it as a general reference throughout scoring.

Scoring Manual Rubric
Grade 8

	5	3	1*
Recognizes and Defines Problem	☐ Recognizes and writes about the science background material that is relevant to the problem.	☐ Recognizes and writes about the science problem but does not understand the relevant background material.	☐ Writes about the project in general but does not include science background material for the problem.
	☐ Proposes a testable hypothesis based upon the problem to be investigated.	☐ Proposes a hypothesis related to the problem to be investigated, but it is not clear how it can be tested.	☐ Proposes a hypothesis that is not related to the experiment.
Designs Problem/ Solving Strategy	☐ Designs an experiment that addresses original hypothesis.	☐ Designs an experiment that partially addresses original hypothesis.	☐ Designs an experiment that is trial and error, not hypothesis related.
	☐ Identifies the variables noting a need for control.	☐ Identifies some variable to test and shows an understanding of the need for control(s) or identifies many variables but control is flawed.	☐ Identifies what will be tested but does not identify the variables.
	☐ Describes an appropriate method(s) for observation and/or measurement.	☐ Describes a method(s) for observation and measurement that partially fits the hypothesis.	☐ Describes a method(s) for observation and measurement that does not fit the hypothesis.
	☐ Experiment could be easily followed and/or replicated. The important steps and materials are listed.	☐ Experiment could be partially followed; not all steps and materials are listed.	☐ Experiment could not be followed and/or replicated. The important steps or materials are not listed.
Implements Problem/ Solving Strategy	☐ Follows the procedure specified in the design.	☐ Partially follows the procedure specified in the design.	☐ Testing becomes trial and error not based on a procedure.
	☐ Organizes and records data using appropriate methods for display (charts, tables, graphs, and/or drawings) including labels and units.	☐ Records data that lacks precision or organization.	☐ Data or the information recorded is seriously flawed with regard to method for display, labels, or units.
	☐ Data is summed up by calculating averages based upon multiple trials.	☐ Averages are not calculated although multiple trials are conducted.	☐ A single trial is conducted.
Interprets and Communicates Findings and Conclusions	☐ Gives a conclusion that directly addresses hypothesis and is clearly connected to observations and/or measurements.	☐ Gives a conclusion related to the hypothesis and attempts to base it upon the observations and measurements, the connection is not clear.	☐ Writes about data making no connections to the hypothesis and giving no conclusion.
	☐ Recognizes limitations of the experiment and explains how the experiment could be extended or improved the next time it is performed.	☐ Recognizes that the experiment has some limitations but does not explain how to improve it.	☐ Recognizes few limitations for the experiment and doesn't explain how the experiment could be improved.
	☐ Tells how conclusion applies to the student's life.	☐ Shows some effort to connect the conclusion to the student's life.	☐ Makes no connection between conclusion and the student's life. Conclusion is limited to telling about something the student learned.

* Use the rating of "0" to indicate that no response was given.

Figure 1.9.

17

Evaluation Guidelines for Process Components

The following matrix specifies the general evaluation criteria for the process component ratings which could be applied to various performance assessments (e.g. projects, experiments, restricted responses) at Grade 10. Use it as a general reference throughout scoring.

Scoring Manual Rubric
Grade 10

	5	3	1*
Recognizes and Defines Problem	☐ Recognizes and writes about the science background material that is relevant to the problem.	☐ Recognizes and writes about the problem but does not understand the relevant science background material.	☐ Writes about the project in general but does not include science background material for the problem.
	☐ Proposes a testable hypothesis based upon the problem to be investigated.	☐ Proposes a hypothesis related to the problem to be investigated, but it is not clear how it can be tested.	☐ Proposes a hypothesis that is not related to the experiment.
Designs Problem/ Solving Strategy	☐ Designs an experiment that addresses original hypothesis.	☐ Designs an experiment that partially addresses original hypothesis.	☐ Designs an experiment that is trial and error, not hypothesis related.
	☐ Identifies the independent variable (the thing that is changed) and the dependent variable (the thing that is measured and recorded). Describes the control which is the constant used for research.	☐ Identifies some variable(s) but lacks understanding of control.	☐ Identifies one variable to be tested showing no control.
	☐ Describes an appropriate method(s) of observation and/or measurement.	☐ Describes a method(s) for observation and measurement that partially fits the hypothesis.	☐ Describes a method(s) for observation and measurement that does not fit the hypothesis.
	☐ Experiment could be easily followed and/or replicated. The important steps and materals are listed.	☐ Experiment could be partially followed; not all steps and materials are listed.	☐ Experiment could not be followed and/or replicated. The important steps or materials are not listed.
Implements Problem/ Solving Strategy	☐ Follows the procedure specified in the design.	☐ Partially follows the procedure specified in the design.	☐ Testing becomes trial and error; not based on a procedure.
	☐ Organizes and records data using appropriate methods for display (charts, tables, graphs, and/or drawings) including labels and units.	☐ Records data that lacks precision or organization.	☐ Data or the information recorded is seriously flawed with regard to method for display, labels, or units.
	☐ Calculates measure(s) of central tendency based upon multiple trials.	☐ Does not calculate a measure(s) of central tendency-although conducts multiple trials.	☐ Conducts a single trial.
Interprets and Communicates Findings and Conclusions	☐ Gives a conclusion based upon the patterns indicated by the data. (An understanding of significance and correlation is evident.) Explains the conclusion using related scientific concepts.	☐ Gives a conclusion partially based upon data and offers a limited explanation of related scientific concepts.	☐ Writes about the project without communicating the data and related scientific concepts.
	☐ Conclusion directly addresses the original hypothesis and tells whether it is supported or not.	☐ Conclusion is only partially related to original hypothesis.	☐ Conclusion is unrelated to the original hypothesis.
	☐ Writes about strengths and weaknesses of the experiment. Generates a related question(s) and/or issue(s) and tells how conclusion applies to the student's life.	☐ Writes about one strength or weakness and generates a related issue or question or tells how conclusion applies to the student's life.	☐ Conclusion is limited to telling about something the student learned, with no mention of strengths or weaknesses, a related question/issue, or the student's life.

* Use the rating of "0" to indicate that no response was given.

Figure 1.10.

18

Scoring Rubric*
Grade 5

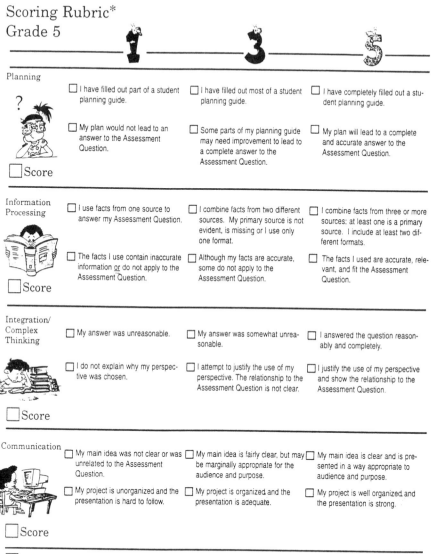

Planning

☐ I have filled out part of a student planning guide.	☐ I have filled out most of a student planning guide.	☐ I have completely filled out a student planning guide.
☐ My plan would not lead to an answer to the Assessment Question.	☐ Some parts of my planning guide may need improvement to lead to a complete answer to the Assessment Question.	☐ My plan will lead to a complete and accurate answer to the Assessment Question.

☐ Score

Information Processing

☐ I use facts from one source to answer my Assessment Question.	☐ I combine facts from two different sources. My primary source is not evident, is missing or I use only one format.	☐ I combine facts from three or more sources; at least one is a primary source. I include at least two different formats.
☐ The facts I use contain inaccurate information or do not apply to the Assessment Question.	☐ Although my facts are accurate, some do not apply to the Assessment Question.	☐ The facts I used are accurate, relevant, and fit the Assessment Question.

☐ Score

Integration/ Complex Thinking

☐ My answer was unreasonable.	☐ My answer was somewhat unreasonable.	☐ I answered the question reasonably and completely.
☐ I do not explain why my perspective was chosen.	☐ I attempt to justify the use of my perspective. The relationship to the Assessment Question is not clear.	☐ I justify the use of my perspective and show the relationship to the Assessment Question.

☐ Score

Communication

☐ My main idea was not clear or was unrelated to the Assessment Question.	☐ My main idea is fairly clear, but may be marginally appropriate for the audience and purpose.	☐ My main idea is clear and is presented in a way appropriate to audience and purpose.
☐ My project is unorganized and the presentation is hard to follow.	☐ My project is organized and the presentation is adequate.	☐ My project is well organized and the presentation is strong.

☐ Score

☐ Overall Score

*(The information in the first column (1) shows unacceptable, marginal work, the second column (3) shows acceptable, average work, and the third column (5) shows outstanding, excellent work. Please remember, scores can fall between columns as a 2 or 4.)

Figure 1.11.

Scoring Rubric* Grade 8

	1	3	5
Planning	My plan would not lead to an answer to the Assessment Question.	Some parts of my planning guide may need improvement to lead to a complete answer to the Assessment Question.	My plan will lead to a complete and accurate answer to the Assessment Question.
☐ Score			
Information Processing	☐ My research included information that doesn't clearly represent the perspective(s) I chose.	☐ My research addressed one of the following perspectives: ___ Anthropology/Sociology ___ Civics/Government ___ History ___ Geography ___ Economics	☐ My research addressed at least two of the following perspectives: ___ Anthropology/Sociology ___ Civics/Government ___ History ___ Geography ___ Economics
☐ Score	☐ I correctly used two or less sources.	☐ I correctly used three sources. One of these is a primary source and I have used two source formats. I have noted these sources in my planning guide or annotated bibliography.	☐ I correctly used at least four sources. Two of these are different primary sources. Two of the four sources represent different source formats. I have noted these sources in my planning guide or annotated bibliography.
	☐ I collected information that is inaccurate or does not apply to the Assessment Question.	☐ I pulled together mostly relevant facts and ideas, but some may not apply to the Assessment Question.	☐ I combined rich, relevant, and accurate facts and ideas that fit the Assessment Question.
Integration/ Complex Thinking	☐ I provided some information but it was not clear how it answered the Assessment Question.	☐ I provided a reasonable answer to the Assessment Question, but only some of my information supported it.	☐ I provided an answer to the Assessment Question which was completely supported and reasonable.
	☐ I attempted to demonstrate how one perspective supported my answer to the Assessment Question.	☐ I demonstrated how one perspective supported my answer to the Assessment Question.	☐ I demonstrated how two perspectives supported my answer to the Assessment Question.
☐ Score	☐ I do not apply my answer/solution to a related real life issue or failed to explain the connection.	☐ I tried to apply my answer/solution to a related real-life issue but the connection was unclear.	☐ I applied my answer/solution to a related real-life issue in my conclusion.
Communication	☐ My main idea was not clear or was unrelated to the Assessment Question.	☐ My main idea is fairly clear, but may be marginally appropriate for the audience and purpose.	☐ My main idea is clear and is presented in a way appropriate to the audience and purpose.
	☐ My organization may include an introduction, body, and conclusion, but the presentation is hard to follow.	☐ My organization clearly included an introduction, body, and conclusion, and the presentation was adequate.	☐ My organization is strong and adds to the impact of the presentation.
☐ Score	☐ My sentence structure and word choice distracts from the idea(s) I am trying to present.	☐ My sentence structure and word choice are appropriate to the ideas I am trying to present.	☐ My sentence structure and word choice create meaningful, powerful ideas.

☐ **Overall Score** *(The information in the first column (1) shows unacceptable, marginal work, the second column (3) shows acceptable, average work, and the third column (5) shows outstanding, excellent work. Please remember, scores **can** fall between columns as a 2 or 4.)

Figure 1.12.

20

Scoring Rubric* Grade 11

1   3   5

Planning

1	3	5
☐ My plan would not lead to an answer to the Assessment Question.	☐ Some parts of my planning guide may need improvement to lead to a complete answer to the Assessment Question.	☐ My plan will lead to a complete and accurate answer to the Assessment Question.

☐ Score

Information Processing

1	3	5
☐ My research included information that doesn't clearly represent the perspective(s) I chose.	☐ My research addressed one of the following perspectives: ___ Anthropology/Sociology ___ Civics/Government ___ History ___ Geography ___ Economics	☐ My research addressed at least three of the following perspectives: ___ Anthropology/Sociology ___ Civics/Government ___ History ___ Geography ___ Economics
☐ I used three or fewer sources. One was a primary source but no sources have a different format.	☐ I used four sources. At least two are primary sources. Two different formats are represented. I have cited these sources in my planning guide or in an annotated bibliography.	☐ I used at least six sources. At least three are primary sources with one an interview or survey. Two of the six sources are represented by two different formats. I have cited these sources using the planning guide or an annotated bibliography.
☐ I collected information that is inaccurate or does not apply to the Assessment Question.	☐ I pulled together mostly accurate and relevant facts and ideas but some may not apply to the Assessment Question.	☐ I combined rich, relevant, and accurate facts that fit the Assessment Question.

☐ Score

Integration/ Complex Thinking

1	3	5
☐ I provided some information but it was not clear how it answered the Assessment Question.	☐ I provided a reasonable answer to the Assessment Question, but only some of my information supported it.	☐ I provided an answer to the Assessment Question which was completely supported and reasonable.
☐ I attempted to demonstrate how one perspective supported my answer to the Assessment Question.	☐ I demonstrated how two perspectives supported my answer to the Assessment Question.	☐ I demonstrated how three perspectives supported my answer to the Assessment Question.
☐ I do not apply my answer/solution to a related real life issue.	☐ I tried to apply my answer/solution to a related real-life issue but the connection was unclear.	☐ I applied my answer/solution to a related real-life issue in my conclusion.

☐ Score

Communication

1	3	5
☐ My main idea was not clear or was unrelated to the Assessment Question.	☐ My main idea is fairly clear, but may be somewhat appropriate for the audience and purpose.	☐ My main idea is clear and is presented in a way appropriate to audience and purpose.
☐ My organization may include an introduction, body, and conclusion but the presentation is hard to follow.	☐ My organization clearly included an introduction, body, and conclusion and the presentation was adequate.	☐ My organization is strong and adds to the impact of the presentation.
☐ My sentence structure and word choice distracts from the idea(s) I am trying to present.	☐ My sentence structure and word choice are appropriate to the ideas I am trying to present.	☐ My sentence structure and word choice create meaningful, powerful ideas.

☐ Score

☐ Overall Score

*(The information in the first column (1) shows unacceptable, marginal work, the second column (3) shows acceptable, average work, and the third column (5) shows outstanding, excellent work. Please remember, scores can fall between columns as a 2 or 4.)

Figure 1.13.

centered learning activities. To address this emphasis, individual student projects have been incorporated into the Kansas Social Studies Assessment [see Figure 1.11 (Gr. 5), Figure 1.12 (Gr. 8), and Figure 1.13 (Gr. 11)].

The goal of the Kansas assessment program is high student performance on test items derived from the Kansas curricular standards. Kansas curricular standards have been defined for the academic areas tested: mathematics, reading, science, social studies, and writing. It is intended that these standards be important components of local curriculum, instruction, and staff development, as well as the focus of state assessment. When local curriculum goals and objectives, classroom instruction, and staff development include the Kansas curricular standards, which match the Kansas state assessments, then "alignment" is achieved (see Chapter 2). This alignment is an important part of reaching the goal of higher student performance. The closer the alignment among all components, the more likely student achievement will rise.

DELIECE MULLEN, JUDY A. NIXON,
SANDRA J. PHIFER, GERMAINE L. TAGGART,
MARILYN WOOD

2

Program Rubrics

Program rubrics are created to evaluate students and school curriculum programs so generalizations about strengths and weaknesses can be identified. During the program evaluation process, standards for judging quality are determined, relevant information is completed, and standards determine the value, quality, and effectiveness of the program. Program rubrics are a systematic effort to define explicit criteria and obtain accurate information about the success of a program. Information from this evaluation empowers educators to judge the quality of school curricula in specific content areas. The information may also assist schools in meeting minimum accreditation standards. Program rubrics are used as formative evaluation to provide program personnel evaluation information useful in improving the programs. They are also used as summative evaluation providing program decision makers and parents with judgments about the program's worth or merit in relation to selected criteria. Summative evaluation leads to decisions concerning program continuation, expansion, or termination.

Our school does not offer traditional grades for assessment. We use a portfolio process with student-led parent-teacher conferences four times per year. Program rubrics were encouraged through our state school improvement process called Quality Performance Accreditation (QPA) (see Figure 2.1).

A method for collecting data needed to make generalizations about student achievement without the use of traditional grades. Considerations began on the possibility of creating school-wide program evaluation rubrics for reading, writing, and mathematics programs. We wanted to plot student achievement at a level independent of grade identification. In this way, we would be able to assess developmental

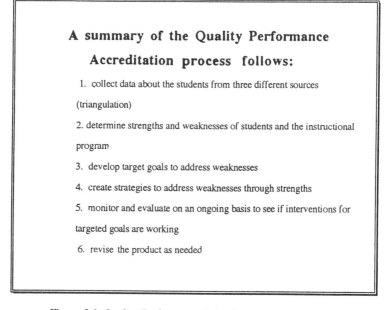

Figure 2.1 Quality Performance School Improvement Process.

levels (emergent, beginning, developing, independent, or fluent) of students. Strengths and weaknesses would then be determined based on that information.

Students collect samples of work for their portfolios throughout the learning process. This might include a K-W-L chart with a final reflection on a particular unit of study or a pre- and post-test on a particular concept. The important element in the collection of materials is that a cover page be included in the portfolio. One type of form used in our school that students place in their portfolios is found in Figure 2.2. Students state why the piece is significant in the "I did a good job on" section and compare it to prior work (pre-test compared to post-test, or What I Know compared to What I Learned) in the "I am better at" section. Finally, students use this information to set goals in the "I need to work on" paragraph. The form is stapled to materials before being placed in portfolios. The power of portfolio assessment comes through the self-evaluation and metacognitive skills that are enhanced through this type of record keeping. It is the students' responsibility to complete

Name: _____

Date: _____

I did a good job on:

_____

_____

_____

_____

I am better at

_____

_____

_____

_____

I need to work on:

_____

_____

_____

_____

Figure 2.2 *Portfolio Reflection (created by O'Loughlin Elementary School staff, Hays, Kansas).*

this reflective process, but teachers may meet with students and conference with them as needed. All students reflect on work in a selected format designed by individual teachers. Our school improvement process (QPA) requires that we collect student information and data in three different ways. Triangulation of data means that we must have three different sources of data and information for determining strengths and weaknesses of students. Traditionally, schools use state assessments, standardized tests, and grades. We could use the first two, but did not have grades for the third. The problem with an alternative grading system is that we have no way to standardize portfolio materials.

We chose portfolio assessment as our third measure of strengths and weaknesses. Portfolios may include performance assessments, authentic assessment materials, products such as reports or artwork, audiotapes, and videotapes. Performance assessments allow students to meet with teachers and demonstrate a skill or strategy. The teacher may keep anecdotal notes (see Figure 2.3) while the student performs a task.

Assessments generally involve students participating in or creating a project and then reflecting and setting additional goals. To complicate matters, each teacher has individual ways of organizing portfolios. In other words, individual teachers use different methods to measure the same concepts with a standard method of documentation. We knew we needed to have a systematic way of reporting results. A rubric for each content area allows teachers to look at portfolio

J.D., 3-15-97, small group writing session

    J.D. is one of five in small group writing experience story about class trip to farm. He drew picture of pig; when S.R. told him he had to write some words about the trip, he wrote, "pig stnk." When S.R. said he had to tell more than that, he noted that pigs squeal but that he didn't know how to spell that. T.W. told him to write the sound that they made; J.D. wrote "ig go EEEEE." He then stated, "Oh, and they like to eat," so wrote "pig lik to et." He then stated that he was done and was going to share his story, so quickly picked up story and hurried to sharing place.

Figure 2.3 Anecdotal Record Sample.

materials and make determinations about individual levels of achievement.

Another break from tradition is that our school does not use a specified textbook series. It is important to understand this component because we measure student achievement in addition to program effectiveness. We use a variety of resources for teaching; textbooks are just one component. By using a variety of resources, we are able to use the best ideas from multiple authorities.

District, state, and national goals and standards provide the basis to create checklists for each grade level. The school district has very inclusive guides for each curricular area. These guides contain sets of knowledge students in each grade level are expected to master by the end of the school year. Teams of teachers from across the district use standards for their respective content areas. The concepts for the individual grade level checklists become the "curriculum" guides. The complete guide and grade-level checklists force educators to select resources and make instructional decisions.

The school improvement process is very localized so that strengths, weaknesses, goals, strategies, and evaluation processes are determined by individual building staff. In this way, the plan can be individualized and made usable. When a staff creates a plan and determines how it works, buy-in occurs. That is the final reason for creating whole school program evaluation rubrics.

RATIONALE FOR RUBRICS USE

So what if your school doesn't need these data? What if you use grades and not portfolios? Why would you create rubrics? Benefits far outweigh the work of creating rubrics, and programs become stronger as a result of careful examination. Rubric construction allows you to have a "look into your school" to see how you are doing. Adaptation of rubrics is recommended, but no school should totally adopt another plan unless it works for your situation. The key at any educational level is the process of determining what is important to your school and then working as a cohesive whole toward the same goals.

CREATING RUBRICS

Once a decision to create program evaluation rubrics was made, the staff split into three teams based upon building target goals: citizenship, communications, and problem solving. Problem solving was chosen as our math goal. The communication goal was addressed because of a recognized weakness in the area of expository text as indicated by analysis of data collected. The citizenship goal provided a way of addressing the need for student responsibility. Staff members chose a team based upon individual interests and talents. Allowing teachers to select a team helped to ensure that everyone would remain motivated throughout the committee work phase. Initially, weekly meetings were held. Additional meetings were needed for some teams to complete the process.

Target goals and strategies were developed in each of these areas to create program rubrics. A sequence of this process can be seen in Figure 2.4. Essentially, each team met, created rubrics, presented drafts to the staff, revised the rubrics based on comments by the staff, and then submitted a final copy for use. Implementation and revision of rubrics was a part of an ongoing school improvement process.

Copies of the district goals and state and national standards served

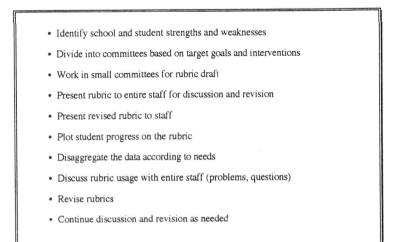

- Identify school and student strengths and weaknesses
- Divide into committees based on target goals and interventions
- Work in small committees for rubric draft
- Present rubric to entire staff for discussion and revision
- Present revised rubric to staff
- Plot student progress on the rubric
- Disaggregate the data according to needs
- Discuss rubric usage with entire staff (problems, questions)
- Revise rubrics
- Continue discussion and revision as needed

Figure 2.4 Steps for Program Evaluation Rubric.

as guidelines for our rubrics. A one-page format design was developed so that all committees had a consistent rubric. This format, with emergent, beginning, developing, independent, and fluent levels, allowed teachers to plot student progress at the highest levels in which all descriptors were accomplished.

The reading and writing rubric we used the first year caused confusion. Some teachers in kindergarten and first grade plotted student achievement at the fluent level, while some fifth grade teachers plotted progress at the beginning level. While this is possible, the subjective interpretation of the descriptors by teachers caused these inconsistencies. Two reasons for this occurrence were considered:

(1) Teachers were not sure what to do when a student could do some things at the fluent level and others at a developing level.

(2) The descriptors were not clear. We found that we needed to revise and clarify to reduce subjective interpretation by individual teachers.

Rubrics are never really finished; you should revisit them frequently as you use them. We decided each teacher must plot the student at the *lowest* level at which *all* descriptors could be accomplished at least 80 percent of the time. There continues to be some subjectivity, but by using portfolio and performance assessments and anecdotal records, reasonable professional judgments can be made.

Having learned that we needed to write very clear descriptors, we began writing rubrics. We found it easiest to write the top level (fluent) first basing descriptors on fifth grade district objectives. We then went back to the emergent level and worked through each successive level (beginning, developing, and independent). Teachers from every grade level, or with experience at every grade level, were represented so we could discuss observations about student learning to guide us. We did not want the rubric to be a grade level list as that would have implied minimum standards. Instead, we wanted to know where students fit on a continuum. We realized that students function at different levels of learning, and this type of continuum allows us to show progress within a developmentally appropriate model. In this way, we are not bound by what students *must* accomplish in a particular grade level, rather what they are *able* to accomplish as they work toward an exit outcome. We still have our grade level checklists, which state the objectives and expectations for learning at each grade level. Checklists are completed at the end of the year and then placed in cumulative records and given to parents. By using a rubric that is not a list of minimum grade level standards, we are able to see how students are doing in relation to peers (see Figures 2.5, 2.6, and 2.7).

USE OF RUBRIC INFORMATION

Teachers plot student achievement on the rubric at the end of the school year. Data disaggregation is done by our building principal and

1997
K-5 Continuum

Student: _____

Date: _____

Teacher: _____

Emergent

During this stage the student:

Identifies own name in print.

Retells favorite stories.

Wants to hear favorite stories read/told repeatedly.

Tells stories from pictures.

Notices/reads print from own environment.

Participates in the oral recitation of repetitive stories.

Often predicts story events or story endings.

Imitates reading behavior.

Beginning

During this stage the student:

Identifies most letter names.

Recognizes that letters represent sounds.

Understands concepts about print: (left to right progression, letter, word, sentences).

Begins to use context grammatical, and/or phonics cues and cross checks with pictures.

Begins to use comprehension strategies with guidance.

Reads independently for short periods of time (Initially about 5 minutes).

Developing

During this stage the student:

Selects a variety of reading material.

Recognizes the importance of and applies the punctuation in printed material.

Self-corrects most errors that interfere with meaning.

Begins to participate in discussions about stories.

Reads independently for longer periods of time (initially about 10 minutes).

Predicts outcomes and constructs meaning from text.

Figure 2.5 Reading Development Rubric (created by O'Laughlin Elementary staff).

Independent

During this stage the student:

Uses a variety of strategies when reading (prior knowledge, word recognition, word meaning, inference, and text structure).

Reads fluently with expression and clarity.

Continues to read independently (15 to 20 minutes).

Makes some generalizations about story elements (setting, character, main idea, story sequence).

Begins to evaluate books using specific story details.

Identifies the purpose for reading.

Draws logical conclusions and comprehends short passages of expository and narrative text

Fluent

During this stage the student:

Makes judgment about literature using critical thinking strategies.

Is an efficient silent reader.

Identifies and reads a variety of types of literature (i.e. biographies, fiction, nonfiction, poetry).

Has a good understanding of elements of fiction (plot, character, setting, point of view, and theme).

Demonstrates an understanding of literary terms and concepts such as metaphors, similes, and idioms.

Understands authors and illustrators have individual voices and styles.

Recommends books to others.

Reads for extended periods of time (often up to 30 minutes or more).

Reads for meaning and uses an outside frame of reference beyond the reading task.

Reads and processes information above the 6th grade level independently.

Comprehends extended passages of technical, exposition, persuasion, and complete episodes of narration.

Summarizes and interprets messages and purpose intended by the authors.

Figure 2.5 (continued) *Reading Development Rubric (created by O'Laughlin Elementary staff).*

school psychologist. Scores are compiled by gender and socioeconomic status. This allows us to see our strengths and weaknesses and go back to the committees to determine strategies needed to meet target goals. We look at scores, see what is working and what is not, and then develop a revised plan.

It is important that the results of the rubrics are shared with the staff to have impact on improving instruction. We make an effort to disseminate data so teachers know how students perform. Graphs must be made and shared with staff to foster success with the interventions and strategies. The discussion that follows the data sharing is an important part of the process to find out what problems teachers had completing

Student: _____

Date: _____

Teacher: _____

Readiness

During this stage the student:

Scribbles as writing

Writes shapes that look like letters

Emergent

During this stage the student:

Draws as writing

Writes letters indiscriminately

Copies print

Dictates notes, feelings, imaginations, stories

Beginning

During this stage the student:

Uses upper case letters most of the time

Begins to write some recognizable understandable words

Uses beginning or ending consonant sounds in invented spellings

Usually writes left to right/top to bottom

Begins to generage things to write about

Developing

During this stage the student:

Can use lower case letters

Begins to use vowels in invented spellings

Uses some sight words

Uses simple, repetitive vocabulary

Uses a limited number of sentence patterns

Writes with a limited understanding of interaction with the reader

Writes with a developing sense of beginning and end

Figure 2.6 Writing Rubric (created by O'Loughlin Elementary staff).

Independent

Writes with a clear sense of purpose

Organizes stories with a clear beginning, middle and end

Frequently uses standard spelling

Confidently chooses writing topics of interest to him/her

Revises after talking with others

Writes in different forms - poems, stories, lists, letters

Begins to organize writing for reader understanding

Writes short, one paragraph stories and expositions

Writes with a variety of words

Fluent

Writes sensory and thought reactions in single paragraph forms

Organizes thought in paragraphs

Includes at least one major idea with details or several major ideas, each with related details

Creates complex, imaginative tales and realistic stories

Collects and uses data on selected topics

Writes comprehensive expository pieces

Employs dialogue

Moves the reader through the text

Conveys ideas and content that are clear and focused

Speaks directly to the reader

Uses words that are interesting, precise and natural with strong imagery

Writes multi-paragraph stories and paragraph accounts with highly involved plots, detailed descriptions and themes

Shows cohesiveness of ideas in sequence, in descriptions and in analysis of ideas

Applies varied forms and style depending on topic, purpose and audience

Is competent with the mechanics of writing

Builds sentences that are strong and use varied structure

Figure 2.6 (continued) *Writing Rubric (created by O'Loughlin Elementary staff).*

1997

K-5 Continuum

Student: _____

Date: _____

Teacher: _____

Emergent

During this stage the student:

Demonstrates 1 to 1 correspondence

Recognizes numbers 1 to 10

Makes a set of objects

Understands ones and tens

Solves oral word problems with manipulatives at the concept level

Identifies penny, nickel, dime, quarter

Counts by ones to twenty

Creates A/B pattern

Names circle, square, triangle, rectangle

Measures objects with manipulatives (no ruler)

Divides objects into one-half and names as such

Understands that clocks are used to measure time

Beginning

During this stage the student:

Recognizes numbers one to one hundred

Adds and subtracts up to three digits without regrouping with manipulatives

Understands addition/subtraction fact families zero to twelve

Solves multiplication and division at the concept level

Understands tens and hundreds

Solves word problems with manipulatives at connecting level (teacher writes numbers for equation)

Identifies coins and their values

Counts by fives and tens to 100

Names circle, square, triangle, rectangle, parallelogram, trapezoid, and diamond

Measures to the nearest inch with ruler

Tells time to the nearest hour

Divides objects into halves, thirds, fourths

Reads a simple graph

Developing

During this stage the student:

Recognizes numbers to thousands place

Adds/subtracts two to three digits without regrouping

Has memorized addition/subtraction facts 0-12

Solves multiplication and division at the symbolic level (one digit by one digit)

Counts different amounts of the same coin

Solves word problems at symbolic level, Can write own number sentence

Writes decimal notation in relation to coin values

Counts by twos, fives, tens to 200

Figure 2.7 Math Rubric (created by O'Laughlin Elementary staff).

34

Creates A/B, A/B/C patterns with variations

Solves perimeter and area with manipulatives

Recognizes a simple line of symmetry

Measures to inch and half inch with ruler

Understands 1/2, 1/3, 1/4, 1/5, 1/6, 1/8, 1/12

Tells time to the nearest half hour & five minutes

Understands the difference between A.M./ P.M.

Understands concept of chance Interprets graphs

Makes reasonable estimates of objects in sets

Independent

During this stage the student:

Recognizes numbers to the millions place

Adds/subtracts two to three digits with regrouping and without manipulatives

Has memorized addition /subtraction facts 0-20

Solves multiplication problems (3 digit by 1 digit)

Has memorized multiplication/division facts 0-12

Solves division problems (2 digits by 1 digit)

Reasons using concepts of place value

Solves word problems without manipulatives, differentiates between strategies (multi-step problems)

Counts amounts with different coins

Creates complex patterns

Recognizes symmetry with flips and rotations

Solves area, perimeter, volume with a calculator

Understands reasonableness of liquid capacity and measurement

Understands concepts of parallel and perpendicular

Measures to nearest centimeter/ millimeter/ one-eighth with a ruler

Names equal units of measurement (3 ft=1 yd)

Adds/subtracts like fractions without manipulatives

Converts mixed/improper numbers with 1 whole

Tells time to nearest minute

Understands the concept of time increasing and decreasing

Creates graphs/charts from data

Generalizes about probability after an activity

Determines reasonableness of result

Fluent

During this stage the student:

Recognizes any number

Adds/subtracts infinite number of digits

Applies different base systems

Multiplies three digit by three digit numbers

Divides four digit by two digit numbers

Understands and applies problem solving strategies for a variety of purposes (multi-step problems)

Makes change in problems with money

Multiplies and divides decimals

Solves word problems with decimals

Understands relationships between fractions, decimals and percentages

Finds and applies patterns across math concepts

Measures angles using geometry tools

Applies concepts of parallel and perpendicular lines

Recognizes congruent figures

Solves area and perimeter of irregular shapes and unknown dimensions

Applies liquid capacity and weight measurements to real world situations

Measures to the nearest sixteenth inch with a ruler

Adds/subtracts unlike fractions without manipulatives

Converts mixed/improper numbers with more than one whole

Understands the concept of time past and elapsed time

Recognizes fair/unfair games

Calculates probability (fractions compared to ratios)

Rounds numbers to any place

Estimates sums, differences, products, quotients

Applies estimation in real-life situations

Figure 2.7 (continued) Math Rubric *(created by O'Laughlin Elementary staff).*

the rubrics and plotting student progress. We discover whether qualitative observations support data.

This process must not end when the rubric is completed. After using program evaluation rubrics, revision and re-evaluation continues. Your document will never be finished, but your work does decrease. Program rubric usage is not about taking pre-constructed rubrics and using them. The process of working through student goals needed at building level, implementing interventions to reach the goals, reassessing, and revising is the power of the process. Everyone must work together as a staff and communicate with one another, building cohesion and communication. Program evaluation rubrics will drive your instruction and should improve school and student success.

Student Implementation of the Rubric

Empowering students to become independent learners is a common goal of classroom teachers. Though the term *lifelong learner* has become an often-used phrase in educational circles, the need to actively engage students in both the learning process and the evaluation of their learning is an important element in creating independent learners. How do the needs of independent learners differ from traditional students? First, students must understand the rules of the game before they can successfully participate. In other words, they must understand what is expected of them as learners and how they will be evaluating their learning. The use of rubrics is especially helpful in preparing students for a learning experience. By explaining and showing exemplary learning, students can become focused upon successful outcomes. The criteria for excellence then becomes a benchmark for students to evaluate their own level of comprehension and the quality of their work. For instance, the Kansas State Assessments are scored using a rubric. Prior to administering the assessment, teachers are encouraged to introduce, explain, and provide opportunities to experience rubric assessments. Only the criteria for a top rubric score are necessary for the discussion. All students are then given equal opportunities to "reach for excellence."

Primary students as well as older students can understand and apply rubric assessments. In my kindergarten class, I introduce rubric assessment to the whole group using an age-appropriate media: drawing. I start by dividing my poster board into four squares. In the first square, I label it number 1 and draw the illustration shown in Figure 3.1.

As students observe my artwork, I ask them if they think it is complete. Their response is usually, "not yet." Next, I number the second

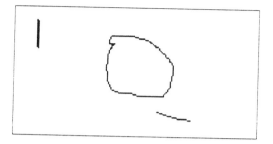

Figure 3.1.

square with a 2 and create the second illustration (Figure 3.2) in the second square of the poster board.

Again, I ask the students if the drawing seems complete. The reactions are not negative, but often not overly enthusiastic either! Again, I draw a third flower in the third square of the poster board (see Figure 3.3).

Many students are now convinced my drawing is complete. I become the challenger to their thinking when I ask them to wait and see my "best effort." Finally, I draw a complete picture, filling in the white space and adding many different colors (Figure 3.4).

By going through this demonstration with the students, they are visually aware of the differences between 1, 2, 3, or 4. We then label each square of the poster with an appropriate number for our art rubic, and the rubric poster is then displayed in the classroom for continual student reference.

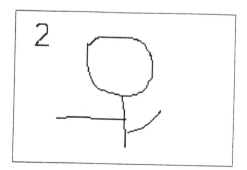

Figure 3.2.

Figure 3.3.

The following day, students are taken through a second exercise to promote understanding of rubric assessment. This rubric is designed to evaluate student handwriting. In the first square of the poster board, the letter shown in Figure 3.5 is drawn.

When questioned, the students note that the "e" is backwards and very messy. A second attempt is made by the teacher as the students watch (see Figure 3.6).

Now the students are able to focus upon the neatness and the quality of the handwriting. Asking for another try, I demonstrate as shown in Figure 3.7.

To challenge their thinking, I again question whether this is the best handwriting I could do. After some discussion, the difference between a three score and a four score is as shown in Figure 3.8.

Figure 3.4.

Figure 3.5.

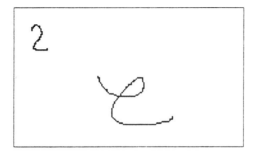

Figure 3.6.

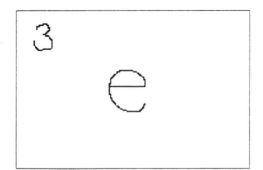

Figure 3.7.

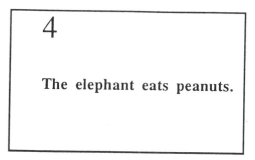

Figure 3.8.

The students were able to differentiate between a three and a four by determining that a three was good handwriting in isolation but a four was good handwriting in daily situations such as journals, letters, stories, etc.

This handwriting rubric was then laminated and is on prominent display in the classroom. The students are encouraged to self-evaluate their handwriting before they turn in their work. Most often, the students will give themselves a valid assessment of their work. When questioned about a three or a two, the students explain why they gave themselves the rating and what they plan to do to improve their handwriting next time. This allows the students time for self-reflection of their work and an opportunity to become active participants in goal setting for themselves. Reflective practices and goal setting are critical elements for developing empowered learners. The self-assessment also allows the teacher opportunity to better understand learners and adjust the instruction to best meet each individual learner's needs.

Whether dealing with primary, intermediate, or secondary students, it is imperative that the students understand the evaluation process. The process of providing examples of criteria prior to assessment allows students time to question and define excellence in their own minds. Confusion surrounding learning expectations should be addressed and eliminated. At this point, the rubric assessment then becomes a working tool for the student and the teacher to utilize together. By allowing students a voice in the definition of excellence, the students develop ownership in the assessment as well as increased understanding of outcomes.

Who develops the criteria for excellence? The national standards provide a uniform overview of excellence for students throughout the United States. As more content areas complete their national standards, a common reference is becoming available to teachers throughout the country. Secondly, as states and school districts develop their own standards, teachers will have additional resources to guide them in developing rubrics based upon best practice. For instance, the *Kansas Curricular Standards for Communication Arts* is written with outcomes, standards, and benchmarks clearly defined. The teachers easily define what instruction needs to take place and define the rubric utilizing benchmarks as well as the broader outcomes and standards.

For example, the following excerpt is taken from the Kansas Communications Standards:

Outcome 1: Learners will read, listen and view for understanding and interpretation.

Standard 3: Learners will demonstrate skills in viewing different types of presentations.

Elementary benchmarks: Learners will summarize and interpret a message and purpose intended by the presenters.

The benchmarks provide elementary teachers with easily accessed, standardized criteria for students. By using benchmarks to define the top level of a rubric, it becomes easy to develop the rubric (see Figure 3.9) for students to become familiar with when being presented with information.

Rubric self-assessment provides natural links to higher level thinking skills. By allowing students the opportunity to measure the quality of their own work, the invitation is given to students to reach beyond their traditional expectations and develop their own personal learning goals and criteria for excellence. All students can reflect upon their own learning progress over time through rubric self-assessment. Designing a rubric with a student assessment form that corresponds with the teacher's rubric allows for one-to-one comparison and facilitates discussion for both student and teacher. An example of such a rubric design is given in Figure 3.10.

Through the conferencing following their rubric self-assessment, students are given richer understanding of the expectations of the instructor as compared to their own standards of excellence. Students are challenged to see learning as something much more exciting than

1	2	3
The information reported by the student is incomplete and inaccurate.	The information reported by the student is complete but contains errors.	The summarized information is complete and accurate.

Figure 3.9.

Technology Rubric, Fifth Grade

Student's Name _____

Date _____

1 not evident   2 rarely   3 occasionally   4 often   5 consistently

	1	2	3	4	5
1. I have utilized new ideas and skills.	1	2	3	4	5
2. I have incorporated many technology resources in my project.	1	2	3	4	5
3. My project is interesting and exciting to view.	1	2	3	4	5
4. My project is functional.	1	2	3	4	5
5. This project best reflects my technology skills.	1	2	3	4	5

Technology Rubric, Fifth Grade

Teacher's Name _____

Date _____

1 not evident   2 rarely   3 occasionally   4 often   5 consistently

	1	2	3	4	5
1. Student utilizes new ideas and skills.	1	2	3	4	5
2. Student incorporates many technology resources in their project.	1	2	3	4	5
3. Student's project is interesting and exciting to view.	1	2	3	4	5
4. Student's project is functional.	1	2	3	4	5
5. This project best reflects this student's technology skills.	1	2	3	4	5

Figure 3.10 Technology Rubric (adapted from O'Laughlin Elementary School, Hays, Kansas).

simply memorizing facts for the test on Friday. Current brain research supports the importance of providing connections and opportunities for reflections as the student learns. This opportunity to experience, question, and reflect is nurtured through rubric self-assessment. Students are clearly aware of the expectations and definitions of successful learning. Now the playing field has become even, with students and teacher working toward one common goal: a challenging and successful learning experience for each child.

SANDRA J. PHIFER
JUDY A. NIXON

4

Rubrics: Setting Criteria for Young Learners

RATIONALE FOR RUBRIC USE

Early childhood educators have utilized many forms of assessments that encourage looking at the whole child as constantly emerging and changing. Rubrics can be created to support developmentally appropriate practices (DAP) for early childhood education. Individual children can be viewed by developmental, individual, and cultural composites of growing and learning. Because learning and development are viewed as being child-centered versus curriculum-driven and teacher-directed, teachers of young children commonly use observation and a variety of evaluation methods and instruments to assess how to structure the learning environment and activities to allow individual children to develop and learn at their own pace and in various ways.

Rubrics fit well with developmental checklists (motor, social, self-help, language), anecdotal records, child products, etc., that are commonly a part of students' portfolios. Rubrics can encourage assessing for individual strengths versus viewing weaknesses; because the purpose of assessment for young children is to determine where the child is developmentally and what the child can understand and do. Rubrics can assist the teacher and parent in looking at the whole child and accepting and planning for the individual instead of viewing the child as incompetent or a failure.

Developmental rubrics include behaviors that reflect development and individual differences in a number of areas. These might include

- language and literacy development
- social and self-help skills

- thinking skills
- individual and cultural differences
- fine and gross motor (Figures 4.1, 4.2, and 4.3)

GUIDE FOR PROGRAM AND TEACHER SELF-ASSESSMENTS

Rubrics can be utilized to help educators assess a variety of aspects about the learning program: the environment (i.e., safety, literacy, or problem-solving promotion), teacher skills, and relationships with parents and community. Rubrics tend to promote more positive attitudes about programs or personnel development while providing goals for future growth (Figures 4.4, 4.5, and 4.6).

USING RUBRICS WITH PARENTS

Early childhood educators strive to involve parents in all aspects of the education process. Both parents and teachers gain valuable information to better understand children's needs, provide environmental stimulation and feedback to promote growth and development, and observe and assess growth and development. Rubrics could also be useful in involving parents in the education of their young children. Some of the uses might include the following:

(1) Help parents understand developmental expectations and accept each child as a competent individual rather than a deficient individual. Parents and teachers can use the same developmental rubrics to provide an extensive view of students (see Figures 4.1, 4.2, and 4.3).

(2) Assist parents in assessing the learning environment at home (language, literacy, social) and determining how they could adapt the home environment to promote further development.

(3) Involve parents in the total learning process of their children by introducing techniques and language that can be used in the home and school to promote continuity between the two.

Rubrics for parents would be similar to those designed for program and teacher assessments. Care should be taken that they are written in

Directions: Observe young child in natural language settings. Check language expressions and responses of child cited below to determine language developmental level.

Early Emergent Language
___ points to objects
___ expresses some wants like "up," "drink"
___ responds to some words
___ uses whole phrase (one-word) utterances like "doggie", "juice"
___ unusual pronunciation makes words difficult to understand
___ vocabulary of 20-200 words

Advanced Emergent Language
___ uses "me," "you," and "my"
___ can form phrases using two-four words
___ begins using pronouns and prepositions, but may be confused
___ applies some grammatical rules (add "ed" to past events or "s" for plurals)
___ asks questions like "What's that?"
___ begins talking with other children during daily activities
___ can be understood about half of the time
___ has a vocabulary of 50-400 words

Early Beginner Language
___ articulation of certain sounds (m,n,h,w,p,k,f,v,t,g,b,d)
___ begins conversations
___ correctly names many objects
___ uses more complex sentences
___ uses prepositions
___ recalls words in a song or fingerplay
___ has extensive dialogue with other children and/or participates in group discussions
___ uses words to communicate ideas and feelings
___ can be understood by strangers 3/4 of the time
___ vocabulary is over 1000 words

Figure 4.1 Language Development Rubric (developed by DeAnna Carter).

47

Directions: Observe children as they interact with print in their environment. Note the attempts made for meaning and interaction with print. Determine the set of characteristics that best describe the child.

3   INDEPENDENT READER CHARACTERISTICS
- Uses multiple strategies to determine unknowns
- Monitors and self-corrects when meaning breaks down
- Understands implied meanings in text
- Has large sight word vocabulary
- Spelling resembles conventional spelling
- Uses capitals and ending punctuation marks

2   BEGINNING READER CHARACTERISTICS
- Uses several cueing systems for unknowns (pictures, syntax, phonetic patterns)
- Can self-correct when meaning absent
- Has beginning sight word vocabulary
- Shows awareness of periods and capital letters
- Uses some patterning in spelling
- Uses beginning, ending and some middle sounds in invented spelling
- Understands the relationship between talking, writing, reading

1   EMERGENT READER CHARACTERISTICS
- Holds book and pretend reads
- Uses picture cues in retelling stories
- Retellings use approximations of booklike language
- Likes to listen to stories
- Associates environmental print with specific places, things
- Attempts to use letters in writing

Figure 4.2 Literacy Development Rubric (developed by S. J. Phifer).

Directions: Use daily spontaneously generated social interactions to observe child's social and personal developmental levels; match child's actions to developmental criteria below.

Early Emerging Skills

___ Is toilet trained
___ Dresses self but may have trouble with buckles, ties, alignment of buttons
___ Tries new foods
___ Recognizes personal property
___ Tolerates reasonable amount of frustration
___ Leaves parents with little or no reluctance
___ Plays or works along side of others
___ Shows pride in accomplishments
___ Can recognize and respond to basic emotions in others

Self-help and Independence Developing

___ Completely dresses self
___ Keeps track of own property
___ Listens to and follows directions with little/no reluctance
___ Helps children and adults spontaneously
___ Perseveres at least 10 minutes on single task
___ Seeks help when needed
___ Describes and responds appropriately to emotions of others
___ Describes cause and consequences of emotions
___ Calms self down

Self-help and Independence Skills Established

___ Works independently without distraction to complete task
___ Responds positively to changes in routine
___ Can find way to/from bus, carpool, school
___ Can work cooperatively as team member
___ Can clearly express problem in words
___ Can realistically view and compare abilities and achievements
___ Can state realistic personal goals
___ Can think of several ways to solve problems or reach a goal
___ Uses multiple cues to evaluate feelings
___ Realizes emotions can be controlled by thoughts

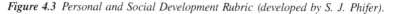

Figure 4.3 Personal and Social Development Rubric (developed by S. J. Phifer).

Directions: Rubric can be used to assess self or skills of others. Numberous observations should be used for reliable and complete feedback. Video-taping is recommended, especially for self-evaluation. Consider strategy mastered if implemented 90% of the time.

Effective Child-Centered Facilitator

___ Circulates and observes all children

___ Gives positive affirmations, interacts and guides unobtrusively

___ Modifies, simplifies, enriches as situation requires

___ Anticipates possible problems; facilitates child interactions to solve

___ Uses "I Messages" to communicate own needs and desires

___ Uses active listening to verify children's feelings, needs, wants

___ Helps children focus and identify problem

___ Encourages children to determine alternatives.

___ Reinforces "child choice" in solving problems

On Your Way to Child-Centered Practices

___ Circulates and supervises all children

___ Keeps adult conversations at minimum

___ Sets limits where needed

___ Encourages and reinforces positive behaviors

___ Organized, consistent in routines and expectations

___ Communicates acceptance by listening to children's view, needs, wants

___ Quickly solves problems between children by redirecting, giving choices

Teacher-Centered Practices

___ Environment structured for safety

___ Children are supervised at all times

___ Rules are fair and appropriate

___ Consequences for breaking rules followed consistently

___ Praise and tokens used to reinforce positive behaviors

___ Teacher responds and solves problem situations quickly

___ Children are told what they did wrong and how to correct

Figure 4.4 *Personnel Rubric: Guidance/Intervention Strategies (developed by S. J. Phifer).*

Directions: Rate the environment and curriculum to determine sensitivity and support for cultural and individual diversity.

3   **High Sensitivity for Diversity**
- ____ Staff and students represent cultural diversity
- ____ Variety of cultural holidays recognized on equal terms
- ____ Visual pictures represent many cultures and races
- ____ Music and foods are shared from different cultures
- ____ Adaptations (activities and equipment) allow all children to participate
- ____ Books and stories represent varying cultures, disabilities, family structures
- ____ Dolls and accessories represent various ages, races, genders
- ____ Choices are apparent and encouraged in all activities
- ____ Children are supported and encouraged in individual expression

2   **Medium Sensitivity for Diversity**
- ____ Little cultural diversity apparent in staff and students
- ____ Various cultural holidays recognized; dominant cultural holidays celebrated
- ____ Most visuals represent dominant culture
- ____ Cultural music and foods shared only on specific occasions (recognized holidays)
- ____ Children with special needs cannot participate in all activities
- ____ Books and stories represent several cultures; limited individual and family differences
- ____ Dolls and pretend play equipment limited in representation of diversity
- ____ Planning for choices not always apparent
- ____ Conformity supported more often than individual choices

1   **Low Sensitivity for Diversity**
- ____ No obvious cultural diversity in staff or students
- ____ Obvious recognition of dominant culture holidays only
- ____ Visuals, music, foods represent dominant culture
- ____ Little or no adaptations made in activities or equipment for special needs
- ____ Limited diversity in books and stories
- ____ Dolls and pretend play equipment limited in cultural and gender diversity
- ____ "One right way" stressed in thinking and doing activities
- ____ Children encouraged to compete for correctness and conformity

Figure 4.5 Diversity in Environment and Curriculum Rubric (developed by S. J. Phifer).

Directions: Log yourself to determine how often you involve your children in the activities which influence children's readiness for literacy (speaking, reading, writing). Refer to higher level to determine future goals.

STIMULATING ENVIRONMENT FOR LITERACY DEVELOPMENT

* Has individual conversations with child every day. Listens when child talks at child's eye level; expands and extends child's comments.
* Acts as speech model; gives objects names, describes actions, uses full sentences, encourages child to ask questions.
* Reads and shares books, poems, songs every day; encourages child to tell stories.
* Encourages play with dolls, puppets, dress-up and pretend-play.
* Points out and reads environmental print: signs, letters, emblems, boxes and cans.
* Involves child in everyday activities: cooking, setting and clearing table, cleaning. Talks about what's happening and why.
* Lets child explore, sort and match objects: canned goods, pots and pans, foods, clothes, blocks.
* Encourages effort with smiles and hugs and loving words.
* Models writing letters, lists, etc.; lets child experiment with writing and coloring.
* Does things together and talks about them: shopping, zoo, museums, library, parks, and other interesting places

AVERAGE ENVIRONMENT FOR LITERACY DEVELOPMENT
* Answers child's questions.
* Uses appropriate speech; talks in full sentences.
* Has books, magazines, newspaper in house; reads with child several times each week.
* Provides child with assortment of toys.
* Reads signs aloud when walking or driving with child.
* Eats at least one meal with child each day; talks about daily events.
* Occasionally takes child along on trips outside of home and care center.
* Helps child feel loved and safe.

LOW SUPPORT ENVIRONMENT FOR LITERACY DEVELOPMENT
* Turns conversations into commands and reprimands.
* Talks to and encourages "baby talk" from child.
* Has little or no reading material in house; seldom reads to child.
* Demands quiet obedience from child when away from home.
* Offers little explanation about what/why they are doing.
* Expects child to play peacefully with others.
* Criticizes child for mistakes or when makes messes.

Figure 4.6 *Guiding Literacy Development: Parents and Caregivers (developed by S. J. Phifer).*

positive terms to provide information that parents can use to make adjustments in their environments and personal habits and skills that will further the development of their children (see Figures 4.4, 4.5, and 4.6).

INVOLVING THE LEARNER IN THE ASSESSMENT PROCESS

In multi-age or nongraded systems, rubrics are assessment methods that are useful for all people involved in the learning process (student, teacher, parent). The goal is to guide individual children and encourage self-acceptance and build confidence in their abilities. Children need to take pride in who they are and what they can do while continuing to set goals to work toward. Rubrics offer suggestions so adults can guide and reinforce development of realistic goals in pre-school settings. In early childhood kindergarten through third grade educational settings, rubrics can facilitate learners to look at themselves in positive ways while continuing to take steps toward their goals (Figure 4.7).

CONVERTING RUBRICS TO GRADES

Early childhood educators who plan for and use developmentally appropriate child-centered curricula include appropriate assessments as part of the curriculum plan (ongoing, child-centered, valid measures of goals and objectives). While these assessment techniques provide valuable information for the educators and students, early childhood programs utilize or require other methods to report progress or achievement to interested audiences. Most pre-school and kindergarten programs use some type of checklist; however, many teachers in the primary grades are required to assign grades to report student progress. Unfortunately, often the parties making these decisions have little knowledge of child development.

Grades, by themselves, do not describe why the child received a particular grade; i.e., developmental differences, variances in background knowledge and experiences, mismatch between learning and teaching styles, neatness, or amount of work completed. Teachers using authentic assessment techniques are faced with the dilemma of transcribing

I can write stories.

___ I know how to edit my writing.

___ I know when to use capital letters.

___ I can use periods, question marks and exclamation points.

___ I can write story with beginning, middle, end.

___ I can write notes and letters.

___ I can write stories with my own spelling.

I can write what I do.

___ I can use periods.

___ I can spell some words.

___ I use capitals to start sentences.

___ I leave spaces between my words.

___ I can spell words with sounds I hear.

___ I can use beginning sounds when I write.

___ I can write in my journal.

I can write.

___ I know some letters for some words.

___ I can write signs and labels.

___ I can write my name.

___ I know how to write some letters.

___ I can write (but no one else can read) and tell about my pictures.

___ I can draw pictures about what I do and know.

Figure 4.7 My Writing Goals (developed by S. J. Phifer).

their information into a grade. There are several ways this might be successfully managed.

- Rubrics might accompany the grade report as a supplement, or information from the rubrics could be converted to narrative form.
- Transferring developmentally appropriate individual educational objectives and activities for each child to a grade may be achieved by using developmental rubrics. For example, if reading was being assessed by criteria similar to those in Figure 4.2, a student might get an "S" or "C" for making satisfactory progress toward their own goals and objectives at Emerging Reading stage. This grade would not be influenced by other students who are working

and are assessed at other reading developmental levels. Use of the rubric allows teachers and parents to consider individual effort and growth, while being aware of where the child was presently operating in the development of the reading process.

* Teachers could design their rubrics to correspond with the number of levels of their particular grading system. A three-level rubric would correspond to systems that use letter grades (i.e., Need Improvement, Satisfactory Progress, and Exemplary Progress; or Introduced, Progressing, Independently Applies), while a five-level rubric would correspond with A, B, C, D, U systems.

An additional problem may arise if teaching utilizes integration of subject matter and grading reports are segregated to individual subjects. Teachers may address this issue in several ways.

* Use separate rubrics for different aspects of the total learning program and apply information from the rubrics that corresponds to skills and knowledge applicable for that subject, i.e., feedback from writing, spelling, oral communication rubrics could be used for language arts grade.
* Give the same grade marking to subjects that were taught as integrated subjects, i.e., social studies and personal/social skills, or science/math process skills.

CONCLUSIONS

Teachers who subscribe and follow developmentally appropriate practices in teaching young children find that rubrics are easily incorporated and serve dual roles. The use of rubics facilitates viewing students as individuals on developmental continuums so that learning programs can be designed for all students to achieve success. Teachers anticipate that at every age and grade level, there will be variability in children's developmental levels.

Rubrics can be strong components of authentic assessment programs. Their use encourages validity and reliability in assessment of process skills in physical, cognitive, social, and emotional areas of development and in evaluating products compiled in student portfolios.

Rubrics provide formative feedback and useful pragmatic information to students, teachers, and parents. As students progress to other classrooms and schools, teachers can readily determine students' levels of development and achievement so the continuum of successful learning is maintained.

GERMAINE L. TAGGART
MARILYN WOOD

5

Rubrics: A Cross-Curricular Approach to Assessment

INTRODUCTION

Authentic assessment engages students in tasks that demonstrate knowledge and skills closely linked to real-life experiences. Such tasks are an ongoing, integral part of teaching and learning. Authentic assessment links assessment and instruction. One supports the other. For example, a teacher observing student use of Cuisenaire rods to demonstrate the concept of equivalent fractions uses the information to establish instructional guidelines. If the child cannot demonstrate the relationship between 1/2 and 2/4, the teacher realizes that additional teaching or reteaching is necessary. Such a task provides the teacher with a diagnostic tool. The task itself is process-oriented, demonstrating the student's ability to observe, compare, classify, and show the relationships that are a part of the concept.

Authentic assessment should engage students in real problem-solving tasks with self- and peer-assessment activities. Additionally, authentic assessment should integrate the activities of assessment with learning and should be driven by standards and objectives that support community and school needs and interests. Wiggins (1993) suggests nine criteria form the foundation of authentic assessment and support the use of rubrics as a viable tool of authentic assessment (see Figure 5.1).

WHAT IS A RUBRIC?

The use of rubrics has become important to authentic assessment activities. Rubrics grew out of the need for more authentic ways to assess

57

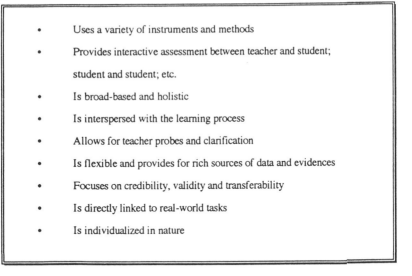

- Uses a variety of instruments and methods

- Provides interactive assessment between teacher and student;

  student and student; etc.

- Is broad-based and holistic

- Is interspersed with the learning process

- Allows for teacher probes and clarification

- Is flexible and provides for rich sources of data and evidences

- Focuses on credibility, validity and transferability

- Is directly linked to real-world tasks

- Is individualized in nature

Figure 5.1 *Components of Authentic Assessment (Wiggins, 1993).*

writing samples objectively with a higher degree of accountability. Rubrics identify and clarify specific performance expectations and provide attainment goals. Rubrics are particularly useful as tasks become more complex and subjective (Custer, 1996). Examples of rubrics include checklists, project contracts or scoring sheets, attitudinal scales, and performance lists.

Rubrics should be clear, easy to use and understand, appropriate to the task, and aligned with goals. Openly share rubrics with students prior to instruction and assessment by providing students the opportunity to create, discuss, use, and evaluate rubrics. By doing so, students experience more empowerment for their own learning, find learning and assessment less threatening, and become more reflective about their learning (Custer, 1996). Learning also becomes more focused and self-directed.

HOW TO CONSTRUCT A RUBRIC

All rubics contain the following components: an identified behavior within an assessment task; quality or performance standard; descriptors of the desired standard; and a scale to be used in rating student performance (see Figure 5.2). Rubrics should define what students know and are able to do.

Assessment Standards

The National Council of Social Studies, the National Council of Teachers of Mathematics, and the American Association for the Advancement of Science have established standards that suggest levels of performance or degree of proficiency expected of students. States have utilized these national standards to develop state standards. Local school districts have further delineated district and building standards based upon national and state standards as well as the needs of the community. The standards provide the core curricula, which aid educators in defining, designing, and assessing content knowledge, skills, and disposition of students.

Task Expectations

Authentic assessment is contingent upon the development of task expectations that support goals of learning. When developing task expectations, five considerations must be made.

(1) The purpose of the assessment must be determined. Assessment serves four main purposes: accountability, program evaluation, placement, and diagnosis (National Council of Teachers of Mathematics, 1989). Assessment provides evidence of the impact of instruction for policy makers and the public. Teachers use assessments to screen children and for placement. Special needs and interests are determined through assessment. Assessments provide data that profile programs and schools, aid in establishing baseline information, and aid in monitoring growth in achievement and equity.

(2) Authentic assessment should be designed to determine the extent to which students can apply existing knowledge of content determined by local, state, and national guidelines and priorities. Other areas of the curriculum that may be assessed are procedural skills, level of reflection, or disposition.

(3) Methods of assessment may include portfolios, pencil and paper

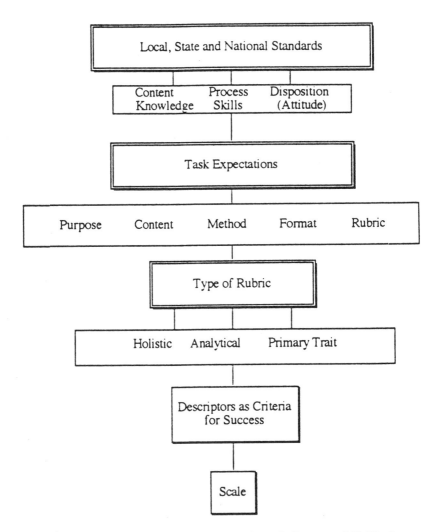

Figure 5.2 Flowchart for Developing a Rubric (G. Taggart and M. Wood).

test, journals, performance-based assessments, computer simulations, and interviews.

(4) Assessment format might be group, individual assessment, or self-assessment.

(5) Descriptors of success and scale should be developed. Students should know the standards and criteria by which they are being judged. Scoring should be done in a timely fashion.

Type of Rubric

When deciding on which type of rubric to use, several considerations must be made.

(1) Determine purpose of the assessment in regard to usefulness to teachers and students.

(2) Consider types and number of goals and standards.

(3) Consider number of students to ascertain which rubric fits the purpose.

Rubrics come in three types: holistic, analytic, and primary trait. *Holistic rubrics* are criterion-referenced, which shows what a student knows, understands, or can do in relation to specific performance objectives of the instructional program. They provide an overall impression and are intended as a summative assessment of the task. Advantages to holistic rubrics are quickness in scoring and its provision for an overview of student achievement. A disadvantage is that it does not provide for diagnosis of individuals. Figure 5.3 provides an example of a rubric that will be used by students to self-assess preparation for an oral report. The rubric could also be adapted for teachers or peers to evaluate students giving oral reports.

Criterion-referenced *analytic rubrics* assess summative or formative performance along several different important dimensions. An example might be the dichotomous, self-assessment rubric of a student's writing process as he or she evaluates, proofreads, and edits final work (see Figures 5.4, 5.5, and 5.6). There are usually multiple parts to the rubric, with each part assessed separately providing for specific feedback for correctives. In the writing process rubric below, the guidelines would help the student come as close as possible to a finished document. Advantages are the diagnostic value for individuals and pro-

ORAL REPORT RUBRIC

After writing your oral report and practicing to give it to the class, check the space in front of the appropriate statements that best describe your preparation.

Expert/Proficient
_____ I considered my audience's interests in my introduction
_____ I used expression in my voice
_____ My content knowledge was apparent
_____ I used several sources accurately
_____ I used clear sentences with good transitions
_____ I was organized and presented information in a sequential manner
_____ I used several visuals to support my content
_____ I learned new facts that I may use after the oral report
_____ I selected information that I thought was important for others to know
_____ I felt well-prepared to give this oral report

Competent
_____ I used an introduction that was interesting to me
_____ At times I used expression in my voice
_____ My content knowledge lacked detail
_____ I used a few sources accurately
_____ I used clear sentences
_____ I occasionally presented information out of sequence
_____ I used visuals without connecting to the content
_____ I learned new facts for my oral report
_____ I selected information which interested me
_____ I felt somewhat prepared to give this oral report

Beginner
_____ My introduction lacked interest
_____ I spoke in a monotone most of the time
_____ I used little content knowledge
_____ I used one source of information
_____ My sentences seemed choppy
_____ Much of my report was out of sequence
_____ I used no visuals to support my information
_____ I learned little new information for my report
_____ I selected my sources and information randomly
_____ I felt I should have prepared more to give this report

Check the term which best identifies your preparation:
_____Expert   _____Competent   _____Beginner

Figure 5.3 Holistic Rubric (G. Taggart and M. Wood).

```
┌─────────────────────────────────────────────────────────────┐
│                    WRITING   PROCESS                         │
│                                                              │
│     Color in the smiley face or the sad face after reading   │
│     each question  below to show how you feel about your     │
│     writing.                                                 │
│                                                              │
│     EDITING MY STORY                                         │
│                                                              │
│     Did I read over my writing after I finished to    ☺  ☹  │
│          see if it made sense?                               │
│                                                              │
│     Do I have a beginning that would interest others? ☺  ☹  │
│                                                              │
│                                                              │
│     Did I say all I needed or wanted to say?          ☺  ☹  │
│                                                              │
│                                                              │
│     Did the ending fit my story?                      ☺  ☹  │
│                                                              │
└─────────────────────────────────────────────────────────────┘
```

Figure 5.4 *Analytic Scoring Rubric for Writing Process: Editing My Story (G. Taggart and M. Wood).*

WRITING PROCESS

Color in the smiley face or the sad face after reading each question below to show how you feel about your writing.

EDITING MY WRITING

Did I check for a capital at the start of each sentence? ☺ ☹

Did I check for a capital on all proper nouns? ☺ ☹

Did I check for commas between town & state, dates, and words in a list? ☺ ☹

Do I have a complete thought in each of my sentences? ☺ ☹

Do I have two sentences running together as one? ☺ ☹

Do I have an ending mark after each sentence? ☺ ☹

Did I check to see if words were spelled correctly? ☺ ☹

Figure 5.5 *Analytic Scoring Rubric for Writing Process: Editing My Writing (G. Taggart and M. Wood).*

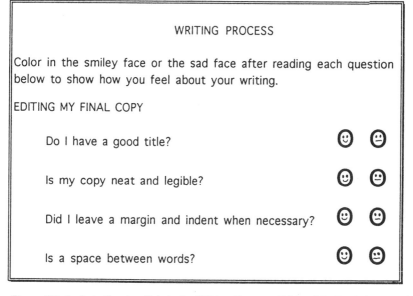

Figure 5.6 Analytic Scoring Rubric for Writing Process: Editing My Final Copy (G. Taggart and M. Wood).

grams and the provision for detailed assessment of the task. A disadvantage is that they are more time-consuming than holistic rubrics.

Primary trait rubrics are established for particular tasks based upon the trait or traits that are most essential to a good performance and are criterion-referenced. For example, a student may be assessed on his or her ability to conserve numbers in mathematics. According to Piaget (1973), conservation is the student's perceptions of number invariance and the degree to which the student is tied to cues (see Figure 5.7). An additional example may be the student's ability to shoot free throws (see Figure 5.8). The rubrics may be used for analytic or holistic purposes and in formative or summative assessments depending upon the format. Generalizations are not possible beyond the particular task or trait being assessed.

Descriptors of Criteria for Success

Once standards, task performance expectations, and rubric type have been determined, teachers and students need to brainstorm descriptors

TASK

Collect eight chips each of two colors, i.e., red, blue. Place eight blue chips in a row. Ask students to place red chips in a row directly below row of blue chips. Ask students questions such as: Are there the same number of chips in each row? Why do you think the number is the same (different)? Collect red chips and place them randomly on table near blue chips. Repeat the two questions listed above. Subsequent tests may involve elongated spacing, adding or subtracting chips, or use of different manipulatives to perform tasks. Use the rubric below to aid in determining the level of conservation with which the student is functioning.

RUBRIC for NUMBER CONSERVATION

Task

		1	2	3	4	5
Mastery						
Student	recognizes rows are equivalent explains rationale for equivalent rows indicates one-to-one correspondence recognizes equivalent rows after 　　change in arrangement of chips explains rationale for equivalence in 　　rows after change in arrangement understands when chips have been 　　added on or taken away explains rationale for equivalence in rows 　　after adding on or taking away					
Progressing						
Student	recognizes both rows are equivalent has difficulties explaining rationale for 　　equivalence of chips in the two rows indicates one-to-one correspondence recognizes a change in arrangement of 　　chips but not number has some difficulties explaining equivalence 　　after re-arrangement of chips understands when chips have been 　　added on or taken away has some difficulties explaining equivalence 　　in rows after adding on or taking away					
Emergent						
Student	can count to eight can set up row of eight chips of single 　　color does not see that number of chips is 　　equivalent for each row does recognize change in arrangement of 　　chips but not number equivalence does not understand when chips have 　　been added on or taken away					

Figure 5.7 Primary Trait Rubric—Number Conservation (G. Taggart and M. Wood).

66

Scale	3	2	1
Position body behind free throw line			
Align toes behind free throw line			
Take comfortable stance			
Relax the body			
Bounce ball in a habitual pattern			
Take deep breath			
Concentrate on basket			
Tune out extraneous interferences			
Shoot ball at basket			
Roll ball off finger tips			
Follow shot with forearm			

Figure 5.8 *Primary Trait Rubric — Shooting Free Throws (G. Taggart and M. Wood).*

that describe proficiency levels of performance. Descriptors are specific observable and assessable behaviors stating what an individual can do. There are two ways to arrive at descriptors that meet assessment needs.

(1) A collection of student work may provide indicators that represent a high, medium, or low performance scale against which other papers or performances may be judged.

(2) Brainstorming or dialogue between and among administration, teachers, and students of expectations serves to provide criteria for success and descriptors of high-level performance.

Create specific descriptors using vocabulary that is developmentally appropriate for the students and exemplify desired performance.

Scale

The final step in construction of a rubric involves deciding upon a scale that will adequately reflect the performance. A scale is a range of scores for each item or task. Scoring scales may be created with two levels, such as a smiley face or sad face for younger children. Scoring may typically use a scale with three or more levels of performance. However, multi-level scale rubrics may also indicate level of performance by using a notice to expect rating. Repetition of tasks aids in establishing reliability of the assessment.

BUILDING A PROBLEM-SOLVING RUBRIC

Steps for constructing a rubric are illustrated below using problem solving as the key goal because of the emphasis placed upon the integration of problem solving into instruction of today's students and in preparing for real-life situations. Students often narrate their thinking processes as they solve problems; therefore, our assessment will focus on the problem-solving process. Polya (1957) devised a four-step process for problem solving.

(1) The process begins by considering information that is important to understand the problem. Discard information that is not pertinent.

(2) Students devise a workable plan based upon information given, prior schema, and limitations inherent in solving the problem.

(3) The problem is then worked by using pictures and diagrams, appropriate mathematical concepts, skills, and strategies.

(4) Student check back to make sure the problem was solved. Reasoning and communication are key components of the final stage of problem solving.

To evaluate the task, a holistic rubric gives an overview of the problem-solving capabilities of individual students. Descriptors are then discussed among students and/or teachers, which indicates expectations for problem solving at the highest level. The teacher and students will brainstorm possible descriptors using the Polya (1957) model. Possible student descriptors at highest level are

• I read the problem thoroughly.
• I reviewed words that pertained to the task, making sure I understood.

- I used all information that was important to solving the problem.
- I was confortable with what I knew about the problem.
- I used appropriate computations, terms, and formulas.
- I reviewed several strategies in determining the best.
- My work was clear and organized.
- I used appropriate terminology and vocabulary to communicate resolution.
- I explained methods for working the problem.
- I checked to be sure that I answered the question.

We will place these descriptors on the scale as a "5." Descriptors help students review the task. While explaining each descriptor, it is acceptable for questions or examples to be provided to students. Keep the rubric manageable in number of descriptors and degree of complexity.

Next, provide descriptors for an average performance by the student. Possible descriptors are

- I read the problem.
- I understood the problem.
- I selected information that was important to solving the problem.
- I disregarded any additional information.
- I computed the algorithms, terms, and formulas.
- I considered only one strategy.
- My work was organized.
- I used appropriate terminology and vocabulary.
- I explained my methods for working the problem.
- I checked to be sure I answered the question.

The rubric is finalized by developing descriptors for less than adequate performance. Figure 5.9 shows the complete problem-solving rubric.

Three considerations should be taken into account while evaluating a rubric: reliability, validity, and utility. Reliability is consistency of scores across evaluators or over time. An assessment is considered reliable when the same answers receive the same scores no matter when the assessment is given or how or who does the scoring. Do two teachers agree on the scores they assign to students? Are students consistent in their performance across tasks?

Validity is an indication of how well an assessment measures what it is supposed to measure. For example, a valid assessment of mathe-

Check the statements below which best describe your performance in solving the problem. Calculate an overall score by determine in which scale (5, 3, 1) most of your check marks fell. If about half were in the "5" scale and half in the "3", you may rank yourself with " 4".

5   _____ I read the problem thoroughly
        _____ I reviewed words pertaining to the task making sure I understood
        _____ I used all information that was important to solve the problem
        _____ I was comfortable with what I knew about the problem
        _____ I used appropriate computations, terms and formulas
        _____ I reviewed several strategies in determining the best one
        _____ My work was clear and organized
        _____ I communicated clearly using appropriate terms and vocabulary
        _____ I explained methods for working the problem
        _____ I checked to be sure that I answered the question

3   _____ I read the problem
        _____ I understood the problem
        _____ I selected information that was important to solving the problem
        _____ I ignored any additional information
        _____ I worked the arithmetic of my problem
        _____ I considered only one strategy in solving the problem
        _____ My work was organized
        _____ I used appropriate terms and vocabulary
        _____ I explained my methods for working the problem
        _____ I checked to be sure that I answered the question

1   _____ It was hard to read the problem
        _____ I did not understand the problem
        _____ Important information was hard to find
        _____ I did not know of any additional information
        _____ I could not decide what to do to solve my problem
        _____ My work was messy; not easy to follow
        _____ I was unsure how to label the problem
        _____ I could not explain a method for working the problem
        _____ I did not check to be sure that I answered the question

Figure 5.9 Problem-Solving Rubric (copyright, G. L. Taggart and M. Wood).

matics problem solving would be to measure the student's ability to solve a problem, and not the ability to read the problem. Does the test support the concepts/processes of the unit? Does the test measure something different than a traditional multiple choice test? Does the test distinguish students who have studied the unit from students who have not? Do students' responses reflect understanding?

Utility is a term that indicates the portability of the assessment. Is the assessment easy to administer and score? Does the assessment provide information that is useful in monitoring instruction? Do assessments improve performance on the end-of-unit assessment?

MODIFYING EXISTING RUBRICS TO FIT INDIVIDUAL NEEDS

Numerous rubrics have been provided in this chapter. It is essential that these rubrics not be taken and used in your classroom without consideration for the classroom culture, needs of the students, styles of learning and teaching, and outcomes you are seeking to assess. It is doubtful that any rubic presented will work in its entirety with your particular situation. Therefore, it may be necessary to revise or adapt existing rubrics to your particular needs. One need for adapting rubrics is to adjust for grade or developmental level of students. Figure 5.10 represents an age-appropriate adjustment to the Oral Report Rubric found in Figure 5.3. The rubric has been adjusted to take into consideration a lower reading and vocabulary level. It is also presented in terms appropriate for a third-person evaluator, rather than as a self-assessment instrument. You should note that the concept and skills have not changed. Any changes in a rubric should be discussed with the parties involved. It is essential that criteria and descriptors be accepted and understood by those being evaluated.

CONVERTING RUBRICS TO GRADES

Rubrics can be graded in many different ways. Some evaluators assign points to each category so that the total possible points for the

Expert	Introduction caught my interest
	Student used proper grammar
	Student used expression in voice
	Facial expressions and movements added to oral report
	Content knowledge was apparent and accurate
	Student used clear sentences with smooth transitions
	Organization and sequencing were evident
	Student used visuals to support content
Competent	Introduction was somewhat interesting
	Grammar usage was sometimes incorrect
	Voice expression was evident at times
	Facial expressions and movement occasionally distracted from the report
	Limited resources were used, but information was accurate
	Sentence structure was good; occasionally lacked good transitions
	Organization was lacking at times
	Visuals did not connect to content
Beginner	Introduction lacked interest
	Grammar usage was often incorrect
	Student talked in monotone most of the time
	Excessive facial expression or movement was evident
	Few sources were used with some inaccuracies
	Sentences were often not clear
	Information was out of order in oral report
	Student used no visuals to support information

Figure 5.10 Oral Report Rubric (G. L. Taggart and M. Wood).

rubric is 100. A percentage is based on the student's performance, and the grade is added to other grades. Other evaluators prefer to assign letter values to the rubric grades: 4 is an A, 3 a B, 2 a C, and so on. One caution about using this method is to make sure that the rubric is written in such a way that 4, 3, and 2 grades represent adequate performance on the task.

Still others design their assessments to follow a pass/fail criteria. In this case, a student passes each topic of the rubric at the specified level in order to pass the course; however, the assessment is not averaged into the student's grade. Students are usually given several chances to fulfill the criteria that they did not pass the first time. Each teacher needs to use a rubric that will best fit the needs of the class and the assessment. The purpose of the rubric is to allow students to know the outcomes of the assessment and to set goals toward the completion of the task.

Numerous grades are unnecessary, especially when using a portfolio system in addition to grade cards. To increase validity, multiple tasks must be scored for each individual. Upon completion of tasks at the end of a nine-week period or semester, use percentages representing several trials for achieving the same task. For instance, if a student used the problem-solving rubric on six tasks throughout the nine-week period, average the scores for each of the trials together, and compare the average to the total for a percentage score that may be entered into the grade book (see Figure 5.11).

Grade Sheet
Problem Solving Components

Tasks	Score Student 1							Score Student 2						
	1	2	3	4	5	6	Avg	1	2	3	4	5	6	Avg
Read problem														
Devised Plan														
Carried Out Plan														
Checked Back														

Figure 5.11 Converting Rubrics to Grades (G. L. Taggart and M. Wood).

Comparisons of scoring scales may be made easier for all those involved if descriptors are written that indicate level of success. Descriptors may be written for letter grades as well as numerical scales or qualitative scales, such as those distinguishing among emergent, competent, and expert readers.

CONCLUSION

Rubric construction and use is in its infancy. Like any good assessment instrument, care must be taken to be sure that the rubric is used in the manner for which it was designed. Rubrics must be compatible with overall goals of the unit or program. Rubrics must measure progress along learning dimensions that are considered important by all stakeholders. Emphasis must be on enabling further learning. Rubric use is ongoing. Evaluations must be made of rubric reliability, validity, and utility. And most important, rubric construction and use must be a collaborative activity based on the natural activities and processes students experience.

REFERENCES

Custer, R. L. December/January 1996. "Rubrics: An Authentic Assessment Tool for Technology Education," *The Technology Teacher*, pp. 27–37.

National Council of Teachers of Mathematics. 1989. *Curriculum and Evaluation Standards for School Mathematics*, Reston, VA: Author.

Piaget, J. 1973. *The Child and Reality*, New York: Grossman.

Polya, G. 1957. *How to Solve It: A New Aspect of Mathematical Method*, 2nd ed., Princeton, NJ: Princeton University Press.

Wiggins, G. November 1993. "Assessment: Authenticity, Context, and Validity," *Phi Delta Kappan*, 75:201–214.

CRAIG S. SHWERY

6

Reading, Writing, and Classroom Rubrics: Ways to Motivate Quality Learning

Do the questions, "How long is this supposed to be?" "Is this for a grade?" and "How do you want me to do it?" sound familiar? Standardized reading and writing test scores have done a disservice to the way many students view the learning process. While standardized tests do have their purpose, students have come to realize these test scores hold more weight than most other types of classroom assessment procedures, often being used to rank their school achievement reading and writing performances. For this reason, many students view performance quality as meeting objectives at the end of instruction (how long is it to be, is it for a grade, how do you want me to do it), rather than before or during instruction. The goal for becoming a responsible learner, then, is interpreted by these students as remembering context facts and skill-based procedures.

While content outcome performance attributes to a learner's academic standing, learning choices must be periodically assessed if that final outcome performance is to be successful. For this reason, most teachers view grades as representative of a "life-history" of learned events supported by decisions a student has chosen (or has been asked) to take along this historical path. Intertwined within these learning events are supporting literacy tools (reading, writing, listening, speaking, viewing) learners use in making practical sense of new information. Regardless of content or subject, literacy tools become the cornerstones to an individual's life-history.

Classroom teachers use a variety of alternative assessments in constructing a grade representing the history of a student's academic engagement. Use of portfolios, anecdotal recordings, teacher-made tests, surveys, classroom observations, book share, retellings, and conferences are some of the ways teachers investigate student use of literacy strategies. The goal for teachers, then, is determining the value of a particular grade for a particular student's performance over time. Because teacher and students have similar goals toward obtaining a graded performance, the issue becomes one of quality. For students, quality is remembering enough facts to receive a passing grade; for teachers, quality is providing students sufficient opportunities to make sense of information to earn a successful passing grade. Assessing a student's understanding means using indicators to verify the quality of understanding and what support may be needed to develop a better understanding. A particular type of reliable indicator, the rubric, sets benchmark goal standards for levels of quality performance both teacher and students can agree upon. Such benchmark standards encourage students to take responsibility for choices and become independent critical thinkers.

This chapter explores some ways classroom teachers can construct these benchmark standards with two literacy tools, reading and writing to motivate and challenge learners in becoming responsible for the quality of their learning, as well as recognizing the importance *process* plays in achieving quality. In this chapter, I use the term *classroom rubric* to suggest the ongoing use of particular benchmark criteria before, during, and at the end of instruction. Classroom rubrics are intended to build upon existing strengths individuals bring to each assignment or project and to challenge their way of interacting with information presented. Classroom rubrics provides opportunities for teachers and students to determine levels of quality attained in their work before, during, and after instruction, which in turn guides necessary adjustments in instruction and curriculum.

The chapter begins by describing how authentic assessment research has led to the development of classroom rubrics as grading sheets for reading and writing. This section is followed by a definition of rubrics, the use of rubrics to motivate and challenge learners, rubric categories, and practical application of reading and writing rubrics. Included within this section is a brief description about current views on the reading process, narrative and expository text categories, and how development of classroom rubrics can support these categories. The next section describes classroom rubrics and the issues around grading, including a discussion of formative and summative assessment, subjective and objective understanding, and converting rubrics to a letter grade. This section is followed by the chapter summary of rubric uses and purposes in classroom assessment. Within each section, examples of rubrics are presented.

DEFINING AUTHENTIC ASSESSMENT WITHIN READING AND WRITIING

Authentic assessment is not a new concept. For decades, classroom reading teachers have incorporated effective alternatives to broaden traditional standardized norm-reference and criterion-reference test scores interpretations of a learner's reading progress. That is, teachers use authentic classroom assessments to help construct a historical view of an individual's reading process.

Included within this rich historical impression, classroom teachers have always viewed dynamic interactions with their students as opportunities for assessing both their own teaching and their students' learning processes, abilities, and accomplishments. Often, teachers and students begin this inquiry process through the use of interest and attitude surveys to establish a link in the curriculum being presented in the classroom. To further facilitate learning and adjustments in instruction, many teachers use alternative assessments to promote collaborative and contextualized independence within literacy activities.

Collaborative assessments require interactions between teacher and student during an evaluation process. While teachers assess student progress in reading or writing, students are engaged in personal inquiry about their own uses of reading and writing. Assessment strategies such as reflection, self-assessment, self-evaluation, and goal setting are effective metacognitive support systems used in building a personal understanding about one's own learning abilities.

There are important differences between each of these metacognitive inquiries (Hill and Ruptic, 1994). For instance, a self-reflection assessment is a thoughtful contemplation of what was learned. Students are presented with a list of questions focusing on affective attributes. For example, "What did I learn?" "How do I feel about my learning?" and "What discoveries have I made?" are questions that can represent emotions and feelings in reading, writing, listening, or speaking engagements. After students have answered these questions, they can self-assess their answers using a self-reflection rubric (see Figure 6.1).

Name: _____

Assignment: _____

Date: _____

I felt I learned	A little	More than a little	A lot
How I felt about what I learned	O.K.	Good	Great
The discoveries I made about my learning were	A little important	Important	Very important

What I Like About My Answers:

What I Want To Change In My Answers:

What Reflection Grade I Would Give Myself (Circle one answer):

1. I spent a little time reflecting
2. I spent time reflecting
3. I spent a lot of time reflecting

Figure 6.1 Self-Assessment Rubric for Student Self-Reflection Responses (generic example).

Similarly, use of self-evaluation questions ("How did I do?" "How have I improved?" "What are my strengths?" and "What are my areas for growth?"), self-assessment questions ("How do I learn best?" "How am I growing?" "How am I functioning in the group?" "What is still unclear?" and "What is getting easier?"), and goal-setting questions ("Where do I need to improve?" "What's my next step?" "How can I help myself?" and "How can you help me?") can be assessed for levels of quality using corresponding rubrics (see Figures 6.2, 6.3, and 6.4).

Name: _____

Assignment: _____

Date: _____

My work on this assign-ment (or project) was	A little	More than a little	A lot
Compared to the last assignment (or project) my improvement was	O.K.	Good	Great
My strengths in this assignment (or project) were	A little important	Important	Very important
I thought areas I needed to grow in were	A little important	Important	Very important

What I Like About My Answers:

What I Want To Change In My Answers:

What Reflection Grade I Would Give Myself (Circle one answer):

1. I spent a little time reflecting
2. I spent time reflecting
3. I spent a lot of time reflecting

Figure 6.2 Self-Evaluation Rubric (generic example).

Name: _____

Asssignment: _____Date:_____

For this assignment (or project): I found out I learned best	By myself	In a group	With the help of one other person
I found my learning growing	A little	More than a little	A lot
My cooperation with others was	A little important	Important	Very important
I identified what was still unclear to me	A little	More than a little	A lot
I identified what is getting easier for me	A little	More than a little	A lot

What I Like About My Answers:

What I Want To Change In My Answers:

What Reflection Grade I Would Give Myself (Circle one answer):

1. I spent a little time reflecting
2. I spent time reflecting
3. I spent a lot of time reflecting

Figure 6.3 Self-Assessment Rubric for Student Self-Assessment Responses (generic example).

80

Name: _____

Assignment: _____

Date: _____

To be successful in this assignment (or project):			
I identified goals and areas I need to improve upon	A little	More than a little	A lot
I identified steps I need to take to meet my goal	A little	More than a little	A lot
I identified ways to help myself meet my goal	A little	More than a little	A lot
I identified how others can help me meet my goal	A little	More than a little	A lot

What I Like About My Answers:

What I Want To Change In My Answers:

What Reflection Grade I Would Give Myself (Circle one answer):

1. I spent a little time reflecting
2. I spent time reflecting
3. I spent a lot of time reflecting

Figure 6.4 Goal-Setting Rubric Student Self-Assessment Responses (generic example).

HOW ALTERNATIVE ASSESSMENTS
INFLUENCE LEARNING

The use of authentic assessments also captures how the roles of reinforcement, reward, and gratification influence learning, which are crucial in the acquisition and performance of strategies, skills, and knowledge attainment (Rotter, 1966). Goal achievement is not a simple "one size fits all" process; not everyone learns the same way, interprets information the same way, acquires information for the same purpose, nor are they motivated to learn for the same reason. Likewise, because reinforcement, motivation, and intention goals influence learning, these same criteria influence reading and writing.

Rather than having our students view learning and achievement as an end product, we can use the same lens to view learning (and reading/writing) as an ongoing, dynamic learning process. Standardized tests should not be viewed as the final evaluation of an individual's success, but rather as part of a dynamic learning process in the "history" about the individual's learning. Moreover, alternative assessments provide socialization experiences that connect classroom learning with real-world expectations that standardized tests cannot provide. Classroom rubrics, as an alternative assessment, concretely support student success in real-world learning by guiding learners through levels of criteria and quality performances. Such guidance helps students move toward higher levels of independent thinking (see Figure 6.5).

DEFINING CLASSROOM RUBRICS

Teachers have used rubrics, especially literacy rubrics, for years. Usually, these rubrics represent teacher-centered objectives for student success in various literacy performances. Classroom rubrics, on the other hand, are intended to move instruction from a teacher-centered-criteria defined performance, to a student-centered-criteria defined performance that eventually leads students to self-assess their own learning. Rubrics are authentic assessment grading sheets defining quality of learning before, during, and after instruction. Classroom rubrics encourage and motivate successful instructional conclusions by defining management and organizational issues relating to instruction. The

Assignment: _____

Name: _____

Date: _____

	Quality	Needs Attention
Format	• Name on paper • Assignment goals and steps identified • Evidence of work in progress	• Goals and steps are weak or not identified • Minimal evidence of work in progress • Owner of paper not indicated
Neat and Clear	• Work easy to read and follow • Assignment goals are consistent with past improvement goals • Graphic organizers and other visuals included	• Neatness and clarity needs attending • Goals need alignment with past improvement goals • Graphic organizers and other visuals missing
Time-line	• Assignment work is at or near an identified time frame • A manageable and logical time frame has been designed • Adjustments have been made to meet time-line	• Time-line needs revisiting • Work schedule needs revisiting
Organization	• Work follows a logical format • Identified goals and steps are included • Final draft represents best work attempted	• Logical format weak • Goals and steps are missing • Final draft does not represent best work possible
Research	• Work identifies multiple sources • Information is accurately presented	• One or two sources are identified • Accuracy of information needs revisiting

Figure 6.5 Example of Assignment Checklist Generic Rubric.

definition of classroom rubrics shifts teaching and learning expectations as end-of-instruction *products,* to an ongoing, dynamic *process* "conversation" between teacher and student. Thus, classroom rubrics allow learners to step back and take a look at their own learning intentions, motivations, goals, and performances (see Figure 6.6).

The Problem	I rephrase the problem clearly	I understand the problem	I do not understand the problem
The Research	I gather, analyze and organize a variety of ideas, options and resources	I gather ideas and resources related to the problem	I gather unrelated information or gather none
The Plan	I develop a clear, detailed plan matching the problem and showing originality	I develop a plan matching the problem	My plan lacks clarity and resources. I execute a plan without considering outside options
The Solution	I identify solutions and show how it relates to the problem. Records are well organized, clear and support the conclusion. I can communicate a concise conclusion	I identify the solution and show how it relates to the problem. Records are well organized. I can communicate a conclusion	I do not identify the solution or relate it to the problem. Records lack organization and do not sort the solution. My conclusion is unclear
The Evaluation	I analyze the process and evaluate how it might be improved	I evaluate the process and note how it might be improved	My evaluation of the process is lacking reflection of what changes I can make to improve my work
The Quality of Performance	My work shows thoughtful progress in my learning and use of literacy tools	My work shows continued development in my learning goals	My work needs improvement and my learning goals needs revisiting

Name:
Assignment:
Date:

Figure 6.6 *Example of a Problem-Solving Rubric (generic rubric for personal investigation).*

Many alternative assessment practitioners who use rubrics understand engaging students in acts of synthesis and higher order analysis
is a strength that standardized tests cannot provide. Consequently,
classroom rubrics are seen as authentic frameworks supporting individual guidance through a dependent level of understanding to a highly

independent level of higher order analysis. As students move through the levels of thinking, they can develop rubrics to self-analyze the quality and result of that work. Figure 6.7 presents a self-assessment rubric teachers and students can use as a guide in constructing their own content-related rubrics.

Name: Group: Date:

Directions: Circle the numbers on the right of each category to indicate overall quality for the category. Next, mark "+" for strengths on the blanks to the left of each quality indicator within categories	1. Unskilled 2. Poorly Skilled 3. Moderately Skilled 4. Skilled 5. Highly Skilled

Works well with others: 1 2 3 4 5
_____ Contributes to the success of group
_____ Allows others to contribute and participate
_____ Resolves own conflicts with others
_____ Displays positive work habits and social skills

Responsibility in group: 1 2 3 4 5
_____ Follows classroom directions
_____ Follows group directions
_____ Uses group time wisely
_____ Meets deadlines (turns assignments in on time)
_____ Limited supervision needed

Uses technology and other sources to complete assignments   1 2 3 4 5
_____ Applies technology in improving final draft
_____ Applies a variety of research sources

Thoughtful in work   1 2 3 4 5
_____ Knows where to seek assistance
_____ Uses higher order strategies to solve problems
_____ Poses questions

Can routinely produce quality work   1 2 3 4 5
_____ Goals are set
_____ Improvement on each draft identified
_____ Final draft represents best work attempted

| Group members response (agree/disagree): |
| 1. |
| 2. |
| 3. |
| 4. |

Figure 6.7 Example of an Individual Participation within Group Rubric.

RUBRICS AS MOTIVATORS

Many educators who teach reading and writing have become dis-
satisfied with present assessment/evaluation methods as a means for
arriving at any true understanding of how well a student can perform
(Smith, 1991). Critical in their dissatisfaction are concerns that standardized assessments are poor indicators of classroom instruction. Most
standardized tests recognize students' successes only on the basis of
facts and sub-skill mastery (Martin-Kniep, 1997). Similarly, many
standardized assessments have not evolved with contemporary research-based understanding of the reading process and fail to capture
today's students' authentic uses and purposes of literacy (Hiebert,
Valencia, and Afflerbach, 1994). Schools and classrooms are restructuring standards and assessment procedures to match more appropriate
authentic indicators of students' reading and writing performances. Part
of this assessment restructuring includes expanding our uses of rubrics
to motivate learning.

Classroom rubrics are powerful learning motivators mapping out
ability beliefs, expectancy for success, and achievement values
(Guthrie and Wigfield, 1997). This mapping helps to focus on appropriately designed goals and expectations between the teacher, classroom curriculum, and students during each level of instruction. These
elements motivate teacher and students to develop frameworks describing consistent, fair, and clear expectations in a particular instructional
learning event. Classroom rubrics empower teachers and students to
collaboratively develop their own purposeful rubrics as instructional
decision-making tools to fit their own particular classroom curriculum
(Fuchs, Fuchs, Hamlett, and Ferguson, 1992; Blankenship, 1985).

RUBRIC CATEGORIES FOR READING AND WRITING

Three broad reading and writing rubric categories—checklist
rubrics, analytical rubrics, and combination rubrics—represent an ongoing collection and assessment of performance indicators during
reading and writing instruction. While each rubric category can have
multiple designs and patterns, all classroom rubrics contain two basic
elements: criteria for assessment and levels of quality. Criteria for
assessment target concepts and instructional goals and objectives for a

particular content or topic. Levels of quality are indicators of quality attainment within each criteria.

The first category, checklist rubrics, describes specific categories that define increasing or decreasing degrees of acceptability for a specific reading or writing task. The level of quality is based on simple yes/no, have met/have not met, indicators (see Figure 6.8 and Figure 6.9). Usually, but not always, these rubrics are developed by the teacher, without student collaboration. Each category is clearly defined for both teacher and student to identify degrees of acceptability. Such rubric grading sheets are often used for a broad cross-section of a stu-

Student's Name: _____

Date: _____

Observation Purpose (initial test, assignment, general observation):

Reading Process	yes	Somewhat	No
Uses of narrative text structure: character, problem, events, resolution			
Self-monitors comprehension			
Is motivated to read selection			
Uses story grammar: setting, what actions are taken to problem, how does action change character			
Self-corrects during reading			

Overall Assessment:

Figure 6.8 Example of Checklist Rubric for Reading Observation.

Student's Name: _____

Date: _____

Observation Purpose (initial test, assignment, general observation):

_____

Writing Process	yes	Somewhat	No
Writes about observations and experiences			
Uses descriptive words			
Edits for punctuation and spelling			
Writing is from top-bottom, left-right, front-back			
Sentences are semantically and syntactically correct			
Expands, extends, or elaborates on major ideas or concepts			
Likes to share writing with others			

Overall Assessment:

Figure 6.9 Example of Checklist Rubric for Writing Observation.

dent's work. However, it should be noted that checklist rubrics are not necessarily student friendly. They are more often used to assess student skill success rather than teaching students the criteria to be successful in a skill. Also, the format does not, by itself, automatically suggest authenticity in assessment because the rubric's categories can reflect traditional teaching beliefs about reading and writing, such as targeting how well students may use phonics in isolation rather than in authentic reading and writing settings. Used as a baseline indicator of students' awareness, checklist rubrics provide information that may be necessary to include or review during classroom instruction or in small group settings.

The second category of rubrics, analytical rubrics, lists criteria of what is expected for a particular instructional assignment. Criteria are usually written in great detail, specifying steps to complete tasks to meet a degree of acceptability. This degree of acceptability, in turn, is assessed for a level of quality (see Figure 6.10). Analytical rubrics pro-

Categories	Criteria	Quality of Performance (check one)
Format	• Identifies topic/project • Identifies descriptions of performance indicators • Identifies criteria • Easy to read; fits on one page	_____ Lack of Evidence _____ Clear Evidence
Communicates	• Clear Standards • Clear Expectations • Clear language usage • Challenges growth • Clear connection between content and assignment • Clear expectations for others to understand (parents, administrators) • Criteria both teacher and students brainstormed	_____ Lack of Evidence _____ Clear Evidence
Reliability	• Language is descriptive and specific • Difference between performance levels clear • Criteria is appropriate	_____ Lack of Evidence _____ Clear Evidence
Practical	• Allows for self-assessment • Allows for peer evaluation • Allows teacher/student to assess performance effectively and quickly • Adaptable to grading scale • Challenging and "Doable"	_____ Lack of Evidence _____ Clear Evidence
Quality	• Clear indicators of quality • Clear indicators of performance • Appropriate for meeting expectations for that particular class assignment	_____ Lack of Evidence _____ Clear Evidence

Figure 6.10 Example of Constructing an Analytical Rubric.

vide clear expectations in a precise and concise manner, and make it easy for students and teachers to reach a mutual agreement of quality performance. The construction and definition of performance for analytical rubrics usually are developed from a collaborative partnership between the teacher and students. As a class, the teacher and students brainstorm criteria each believes represents appropriate performance for a finished project. These criteria are then labeled with quality indicators supporting various degrees of success with the assignment or project.

The third category of rubrics, combination rubrics, combines checklist rubrics with the more detailed analytical rubrics (see Figure 6.11). Combination rubrics provide the greatest detail of a learner's progress through the classroom curriculum. Because of the nature of these rubrics, both teacher and student can assess how a variety of strategies was applied to reach a particular level of acceptability and quality. Also, these rubrics are much more student-centered and challenge students to use strategies and skills practiced in other assignments in new and different ways. As the combination rubric example suggests, this category of rubrics enables a cascading effect from past rubric categories by communicating higher quality expectations.

Each rubric category provides both the teacher and student an informed and authentic assessment of progress, strengths, and opportunities to develop self-assessment quality learning. That is, checklist, analytical, and combination rubrics can encourage individual metacognitive and metacomprehension awareness as instruction moves through a particular content. In the next section, readers will see how closely current reading theories resemble this metacognitive and metacomprehension development.

THE READING PROCESS

Reading theories and their corresponding methods can be grouped into three theoretical categories (Harste, 1985): (1) The Information Transmission theory and methods supporting a skill-based understanding about the reading process; (2) The Interaction theory and methods supporting a skill-based and rule-based understanding about the reading process and; (3) The Transaction theory and methods supporting a constructivist meaning-making understanding about the reading process.

Writing Presentation

Goals of Writing Presentation:

* Writes an introduction which includes a statement of the main idea or theme and writes a summarizing paragraph.
* Develops the main idea or theme with appropriate and accurate examples and other support resources.
* Well-organized, logical paragraphs with clear transition sentences between each new supporting thought.
* Research and other supporting resources understood and clearly stated in author's own words.
* Final draft shows content development from each previous draft.

What to do for an **A**:

1. Precise standard words, sentences
2. All necessary detail for reader to make sense of written paper
3. Effective organization
4. Writing is clear, accurate, and interesting
5. Includes multiple research sources
6. Final draft is edited for spelling and other grammar usage

What to do for a **B**:

1. Clear standard words, sentences
2. Easily grasped information
3. Clear and to the point in message
4. Central point first and in logical order
5. Organized
6. Contains several references
7. Final draft is edited but still contains some errors

A student will be marked "**N**" if final draft is:

1. Hard to follow and awkward
2. Does not have completed thoughts
3. Contains repetitive information
4. Is in illogical order
5. Is missing a central point
6. Is missing reference sources
7. Is lacking any editing

Students who receive an "**N**" will be expected to continue work on assignment until they have achieved either an "**A**" or a "**B**".

Figure 6.11 *Example of Outline for Combination Rubric.*

Early reading theorists envisioned the reading process as a fact-gathering skill where information was being transmitted from sone "expert source" to a learner of that information. Hence, the Information Transmission skilled-based reading theories propose that one "teaches" reading in hierarchical, separate, isolated decoding skills. A reading term, bottom-up, is most often associated with this type of reading belief. Bottom-up reading suggests the text brings to the reader all necessary information needed for comprehension to effectively occur. A reader with proficient decoding skills would, according to this theory, be a proficient reader.

Later reading theorists accompanied cognitive learning theorists to scaffold how we read and what we do with the information we do read. These theorists suggested the reading process was dependent on what the reader could bring to a reading activity and advocated the Interaction rule-based reading theory, which combined the bottom-up process with a top-down reading process—what the reader brings to the text. Hence, a back-and-forth interaction occurs between the text and what the reader knows about reading (strategies, rules) and the reader's prior experiences and knowledge with the text's information. The reader would continually adjust and change personal understanding to fit this back-and-forth interaction. In this theory, a reader who develops rich prior knowledge from school-related and nonschool-related experiences would have greater proficiency in his or her reading.

Most contemporary reading theorists suggest the reading process is far more complex than dependency upon skills, rules, and on a reader's prior knowledge and experiences. These theorists advocate the reader brings to a literacy experience a rich sociopsycholinguistic understanding that influences comprehension. The Transactional constructed meaning-making based reading theory suggests a constructed transaction occurs between the reader and a text each time the reader encounters a text. This transaction is different from past reading theories and has far-reaching importance. For example, the interaction reading theories suggest a change in understanding occurs during reading; the transaction theories suggest an exchange occurs between a reader and a text where individual interpretations about the information are developed. An individual's social and cultural beliefs and practices, learning intentions, motivations, goals, past experiences, and knowledge are all elements that influence the comprehension outcome when engaged with text. Individuals who embrace this theory view reading as an activity that is learned, not taught. One learns to read by reading more. From this point of view, knowledge cannot be unlearned. Rather knowledge is transitioned into a different understanding, while still containing all the "pieces" learned up to that point. One becomes more knowledgeable about the physical, social, emotional environment around them—a lifelong learning process.

Just as reading theories have been grouped into categories, all printed material can be grouped into two broad categories: narrative text and expository text. Narrative text readings, such as stories, are the most familiar and most practiced text because all sociocultural beliefs and practices are told through stories. Most informal reading inventories (IRI) and other opportunities to gauge a reader's understanding and reading ability use narrative text.

Narrative texts have specific elements to a story's framework—setting, characters, plot, conflict, and resolution are some of the basic elements. Story elements are usually assessed through story maps and story frames strategies. Story maps and story frames are appropriate examples most teachers use to teach story elements and assess how a reader uses these elements to acquire an understanding of the information in a story. Classroom rubrics can be used to assess the performance quality level of an individual's comprehension (see Figure 6.12).

Expository text information is usually nonfiction material in origin and has traditionally been difficult for all school-age readers to effectively comprehend. The greatest hindrance in comprehension comes not because students can't read but rather because of the lack of familiarity and practice with expository text. Most readers are so familiar with how to read narrative text and the purpose in reading this category of text that they believe this to be the way all text should be approached. With this in mind, it is possible to be a good reader of narrative text and a poor reader of expository text.

An important distinction of expository text is the purpose for the material and how the material should be read. It is my belief the earlier we introduce our young readers to informational text, the earlier we can develop strong research and study habits. Unlike narrative text, expository text is meant to be studied. Readers of expository text should always have a defined purpose for reading with posed questions driving motivation in reading the text. Through sufficient exposure and practice with expository text, a reader will recognize the differences in purpose and reading fluency rate between the two categories of text. Classroom expository-related rubrics are excellent scaffolding systems to set purposes for reading informational material.

CLASSROOM RUBRICS AND GRADING

Alternative assessment rubrics contextualize learning; that is, information collected from classroom life draws upon data that are rich,

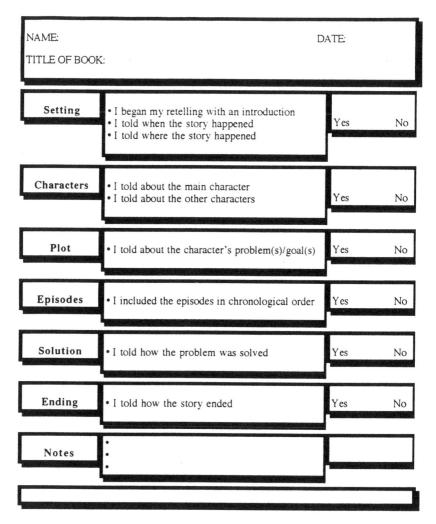

Figure 6.12 *Example of Story Frame Retelling Checklist Rubric.*

varied, and ongoing examples of day-to-day learning (Weaver, 1994). These formative collections accompany clear, descriptive performance criteria that convey understandable expectations for students, teachers, parents, and administrators (Martin-Kniep, 1997). Such performance criteria justify and defend the validity and reliability standards teachers value to reach exemplar work.

Traditionalists have criticized the reliability and validity of alternative assessments and corresponding rubrics as assumptions about an individual. Suffice it to say, critics for and against alternative assessment have conducted and continue to conduct studies in regard to this controversy. These works have led to important distinctions between assessment and evaluation, between formative and summative, and between subjectivity and objectivity when it comes to grading an individual's performance quality. Evaluation usually refers to the process where a teacher analyzes and interprets data to determine the extent to which students are achieving instructional objectives (Gronlund, 1985). Assessment is the gathering of data, usually quantitative in nature and based on testing, that provide the information for evaluation to be made (Bertrand, 1993). These two terms have been used interchangeably in most classrooms when discussing students' scores.

The controversies abound regarding the types of testing to be used. Standardized tests fall into two categories: norm-referenced and criterion-referenced. Norm-referenced tests provide a measure of performance between a student's performance standing with some other known group; for instance, comparison between a fifth grader and all other fifth graders in a state. Thus, a student scoring at the 85th percentile in reading earned a score exceeding 85 percent of the students in the comparison group. Criterion-referenced tests provide a measure of performance in clearly defined and narrow domains of learning to which the test giver knows (not assumes) the learner has been exposed. These tests identify strengths and weaknesses in knowledge and performance.

These testing practices rest on an assumption about evaluation — objective testing is the most appropriate and reliable means of arriving at an evaluation of student performance. As I mentioned at the beginning of the chapter, this assumption translates to mean knowledge of facts is the most important goal in grading and evaluating. This assumption is being questioned by most classroom teachers as they reach the conclusion that few students are successful in higher order critical analysis of what they know and don't know.

The scientific assumption about evaluation leads to another assumption about standardized testing, that of subjectivity and objectivity. Traditional testing advocate teachers should not be allowed to depend on their own judgment in evaluating their students. Teachers have been encouraged to engage in objective testing that does not include their own professional interpretations in the process of evaluating the student. The assumption suggests classroom teachers, if left to interject their own interpretation, albeit professionally biased, would "muddy" the results with "subjective" opinions.

However, what classroom teachers have known for decades and are voicing through uses of alternative assessments is standardized "objectives" measure lower order thinking performance. Teachers know learning components are quite complex and one type of testing cannot measure all of these components authentically. Issues of ability, what is developmentally appropriate, biologically ready learners, interest, motivations, goals, cultural differences, and diversity among learners each suggest students do not come to class as potential equals, as standardized tests propose.

It is true teachers are subjective in their evaluations and grading of individual students. But these subjective indicators are professionally informed opinions of performance quality. Assessments such as rubrics measure the distance an individual has grown in a way standardized testing cannot. Rubrics are subjective in that both teacher and student determine important goals learners need to reach on that particular assignment or project. Once these indicators are established, they become objective indicators for all students to reach. For example, a student may have performed poorly during one particular assignment, the rubric verifying this performance, while most other students did better. The next time the student performs on a similar assignment, the rubric indicates considerable improvement. An objective assessment grade can be converted from these performance indicators (see Figure 6.13). An evaluation grade that includes alternative assessment data will reveal this movement in growth to a wider audience.

Classroom rubrics as grading sheets support performance by identifying qualities students are expected to reach (see Figure 6.14). These scoring guides challenge students to self-assess their own learning by providing concrete information of where they stand in their work. The rubrics presented in this chapter, except checklists, allow the student to self-analyze their learning and set goals for improvement based on performance levels. As these goals are met, classroom rubrics are altered to challenge further goal-setting achievements. Purposes, motivations, intentions, and what is developmentally appropriate are all part of this process.

The following criteria represents levels of assessment for I - Search paper project. While the levels move between 1 (representing a grade of "D") and 4 (representing a grade of "A"), *quality* of attainment between and among each level is *always* a guiding factor during any alternative assessment. The final draft turned in must be typed, double spaced, and on *one* side of the paper only.

Level 4: I- Search paper includes
• A positive narrative tone throughout the writing.
• A reflective analysis of the paper's outcome.
• A summary containing group members' self-evaluation of what was learned from the experience.

Level 3: I - Search paper includes
• An informative summation about the personal importance for pursuing the chosen topic.
• Writing representing a clear, organized picture of the process in researching the topic.

Level 2: I - Search paper includes
• Writing that is understandable, organized and makes sense.
• Writing representing an acceptable form; edited for spelling, sentence structure, correct usage of tenses.
• A final draft presenting a variety of resources.
• A final draft describing information about the paper's topic.

Level 1: I - Search paper includes
• A conceptual graphic organizer that represents the paper's topic
• General, vague topic.
• Record of group participation (journal, log).
• A final draft that is more than **three** pages in length.

Figure 6.13 *Example of Scoring Guide for I-Search Paper.*

NOTE: Not every scoring criteria for all possible indicators are described in this guide. For some activities, the scale will shift to meet the performance indicators.

O = Little or no evidence of construction of meaning. Presence of some indefensible information.

1 = A superficial understanding of the text, with evidence of meaning construction. One or two relevant but unsupported inferences.

2 = A developing understanding of the text with evidence of connections, extensions, or examination of the meaning. Connections among the reader's ideas and the text are implied. Extensions and examinations are related to the text but explicit references to the text in support of inferences are not present. When more than one stance is possible, the response may be limited to one stance.

3 = A developed understanding of the text with evidence of connections, extensions, examinations of meaning and defense of interpretations. Connections among the reader's ideas and the text itself are explicit. Extensions and examination are accompanied by explicit references to the text supporting the inferences. If necessary, responses indicate more than two stances, all substantially supported by references to the text.

4 = A complex, developed understanding of the text with evidence of connections, extensions, examinations of meaning, and defense of interpretations. Connections among the reader's ideas and the text itself are explicit. Extensions and examinations are accompanied by explicit reference to the text in support of inferences. Responses indicate as many stances as possible based on the activity, all substantially supported by references to the text. These responses reflect careful thought and thoroughness.

GRADING CODE:

O = No grade; not acceptable

1 = D; The writer's responses are off task. Need to revisit goals and performance criteria

2 = C; The writer's responses are developing. Goals and performance criteria are improving

3 = B; The writer's responses are explicit. Most goals and performance criteria are met.

4 = A; The writer's responses are complex. All goals and performance criteria are met.

Figure 6.14 *Example of a Scoring Rubric Guide for Reading.*

SUMMARY

Clear performance standards provide students, teachers, parents, and administrators with an understanding of what teachers and students value as important indicators to reach exemplary work. Such performance standard criteria also justify and defend the validity and reliability of grades.

Classroom-developed rubrics represent a dramatic change from traditional testing and evaluation practices and will move education away from test-driven measures to student-centered observation. Each category of rubrics has the potential to move instruction and learning to be more objectively authentic and consistent. Rubrics also involve students in taking responsibility for scoring and maintaining their own learning growth.

However, as with any assessment, a caveat about rubrics: Quality rubrics take time to develop to be effective and challenging. Rubrics do have the potential to reduce information-rich activities to a selected set of easily observable behaviors. Important learning criteria may be the most difficult to document and incorporate into the rubric structure (Custer, 1996). The challenge of developing good rubrics to incorporate important learning indicators such as problem posing and problem solving, critical thinking, and transitional learning needs to be prefaced with purpose of instruction and assessment. Finally, rubrics are one of many assessment tools that should be developed and used to assess learners.

REFERENCES

Bertrand, J. E. 1993. "Student Assessment and Evaluation." In *Assessment and Evaluation in Whole Language Programs*, B. Harp, ed., Norwood, MA: Christopher-Gordon Publishers, Inc., pp. 19–35.

Blankenship, C. S. 1985. "Using Curriculum-Based Assessment Data to Make Instructional Decisions," *Journal of Exceptional Children*, 52(3):233–238.

Custer, R. L. 1996. "Rubrics: An Authentic Assessment Tool for Technology Education," *The Technology Teacher Journal*, 55(4):27–37.

Fuchs, L. S., D. Fuchs, C. L. Hamlett and C. Ferguson. 1992. "Within Curriculum-Based Measurement: Using a Reading Maze Task," *Journal of Exceptional Children*, March/April:436–449.

Gronlund, N. 1985. *Measurement and Evaluation in Teaching*, 5th edition, New York, NY: Macmillan Publishing Company.

Guthrie, J. T. and A. Wigfield. 1997. "Reading Engagement: A Rationale for Theory and Teaching." In *Reading Engagement: Motivating Reading through Integrated Instruction*, J. Guthrie and A. Wigfield, eds., Newark, DE: International Reading Association, pp. 1–12.

Harste, J. C. 1985. "Portrait of a New Paradigm: Reading Comprehension Research." In *Landscapes: A State-of-the-Assessment of Reading Comprehension Research*, A. Crismore, ed., Bloomington: Indiana University, pp. 1–24.

Hiebert, E. H., S. W. Valencia and P. P. Afflerbach. 1994. "Definitions and Perspectives." In *Authentic Reading Assessment: Practices and Possibilities*, S. Valencia, E. Hiebert and P. Afflerbach, eds., Newark, DE: International Reading Association, pp. 1–4.

Hill, B. C. and C. Ruptic. 1994. *Practical Aspects of Authentic Assessment: Putting the Pieces Together,* Norwood, MA: Christopher-Gordon Publishers, Inc.

Martin-Kniep, G. 1997. "Implementing Authentic Assessment in the Classroom, School, and School District." In *Literacy Portfolios: Using Assessment to Guide Instruction,* R. B. Wiener and J. H. Cohen, eds., Upper Saddle River, NJ: Prentice-Hall, Inc., pp. 240–259.

Rotter, J. B. 1966. "Generalized Expectancies for Internal versus External Control of Reinforcement," *Psychological Monographs,* 80:1–28.

Smith, M. L. 1991. "Put to the Test: The Effects of External Testing on Teachers," *Educational Researcher,* 20(5):8–11.

Weaver, C. 1994. "Children's Motivations for Reading and Reading Engagement." In *Reading Engagement: Motivating Reading through Integrated Instruction,* J. Guthrie and A. Wigfield, eds., Newark, DE: International Reading Association, pp. 14–33.

Using Rubrics in Specialty Areas

Rubrics are so versatile that their use is almost limitless. They can be adapted to conform to all age, developmental, and competency levels in numerous subjects and topic areas to facilitate the assessment processes for broad or specific skills, attitudes, or behaviors. Rubrics are particularly suited in a number of specialty areas, e.g., music, physical education, drama, speech, art, home economics.

Rubrics are beneficial in heightening the validity and reliability factors of assessment. The process of constructing a rubric requires teachers to clarify and define expectations. Rubrics can be developed to guide the processes (for teacher or other individuals who are charged with "judging" responsibility) of sorting or selecting students for special roles or parts, or for determining placements or grades. When rubrics are shared with or formed jointly with students during the formative stages of the learning processes, students can set goals and determine specific behaviors or attitudes to target for further effort and growth. Rubrics also serve as a communication enhancer with parents who desire information on the progress of their children.

DEVELOPING A RUBRIC FOR STORYTELLING

Students are asked to tell or retell stories for a variety of reasons. Students may be asked to tell or retell a story to determine if they understood concepts about the story, i.e., sequencing, parts of a story, cause-effect. One might also assess their verbal skills and understanding of how enunciation, volume, and nonverbal language enhance the communication between the speaker and audience. More advanced students, for example, those in drama or communications classes, would undoubtedly have expanded expectations.

The teacher might start the process by listing the behaviors expected from students while telling stories. These behaviors would include aspects of knowing the story and communication skills in sharing the story with the audience. In beginner or young children, the teacher would model a storyteller using skills expected of the students at the highest level. To further students' understanding of expectations, the teacher should model the middle and beginner levels and encourage students to determine the differences in storytellers' behaviors and the enjoyment of the story by the audience. Young or less-experienced storytellers and listeners would find a simplified rubric version easier to understand and use (see Figure 7.1).

More experienced and higher level students would have more inclusive expectations.

Teacher's list of expected storytelling skills:

- introduction that provides motivation to listen
- story appropriate for age-level of audience
- transitions between sequence of events
- props to enhance story (if needed)

Name: _____

	Yes	Sometimes	No
Introduced the story			
Talked clearly			
Made audience "feel" story			
Knew the story			

Figure 7.1 Student Storytelling Rubric.

- correct usage of grammar
- inclusion of dialogue
- descriptive language
- clear enunciation
- appropriate gestures/body language
- facial excitement
- varied dynamics
- correct usage of timing
- motives/conflicts/values of story
- story conclusion
- story committed to memory

The teacher could then work with students to differentiate between levels of competence or expertise in telling the story. Students would then be able to clarify skills and behaviors that they were expected to demonstrate during their storytelling experience and understand the difference between levels of competency. A follow-up could be to participate as observer and rater for their own and classmates' storytelling events. This could be accomplished live or by videotaping students' storytelling.

It would be easiest to describe three levels of competency (Figure 7.2). Discussing and clarifying expected behaviors, highest expectations could be listed as Level 1. Level 5 could describe the beginner who still needs work to successfully communicate the story to the audience, and Level 3 would describe a person who was effective in some but not all skills. If additional levels were desired, one could assign a level between 1 and 3 and 5 for students who demonstrated some skills from each of the two levels.

PHYSICAL EDUCATION USES

Physical education programs address goals and objectives that focus toward developing physical skills and understanding concepts of wellness, health, and safety factors. Exhibiting attitudes and behaviors toward respect, cooperation, trust, and teamwork are also important in the physical education areas. Rubrics could be developed to measure progress in all these areas; however, they could be most useful to students in the areas of physical skills and affective attitudes and behaviors (see Figures 7.3 and 7.4).

Check the behaviors that best describes the storyteller. If the storyteller uses some from two of the sets (or few from third), circle the number between the two sets (bottom of page).

Set 1 Behaviors

___ Provides motivating introduction
___ Uses transitions between sequence of events
___ Uses props to enhance story (if needed)
___ Uses correct grammar (or appropriate to character)
___ Includes dialogue of characters
___ Includes descriptive language to enhance visual images
___ Speaks with clear enunciation
___ Uses appropriate gestures/body language
___ Uses facial excitement
___ Uses varied dynamics
___ Uses timing correctly
___ Conveys motives/conflicts/values
___ Uses conclusion
___ Selects story appropriate for audience
___ Knows the story

Set 3 Behaviors

___ Uses introduction, but doesn't motivate to listen
___ Uses some transitions between sequence of events
___ Uses props (if needed)
___ Uses incorrect grammar at times
___ Includes little dialogue
___ Includes some descriptive language
___ Uses slang that was not related to character
___ Uses words with shortened/deleted prefixes or suffixes, not character related
___ Uses some appropriate gestures/body language
___ Uses some facial excitement
___ Varies vocal expression and dynamics sometimes
___ Uses some correct timing
___ Expresses clear motive/conflicts, values at times
___ Finishes with conclusion
___ Uses story appropriate for age level

Set 5 Behaviors

___ Lacks introduction
___ Uses no transitions between sequence of events
___ Uses no supportive props
___ Uses incorrect grammar
___ Includes little or no dialogue
___ Uses little or no descriptive language
___ Enunciates unclearly
___ Uses few, if any, gestures/body language
___ Uses expressionless face
___ Uses monotone voice
___ Use of timing ineffectively
___ Conveys no motives/conflicts/values
___ Stumbles or forgets story
___ Selects inappropriate story for listeners

OVERALL COMPETENCY LEVEL: 1 2 3 4 5

Figure 7.2 *Storytelling Rubric (created by Mary Meckenstock).*

Looks Like	Sounds Like
Dressed in activity clothes	
In ready position/spot	Quiet
Waiting turn	Go ____!
Smiling face	Good try!
	You'll get it next time.
Pat on back	I'm getting closer.

Figure 7.3 Example of Students' Responses.

Directions: Observe student during class; select the set of behaviors that best describe the individual.

Level 5:
- Is on time and ready to participate
- Is in proper space/place at assigned time
- Shows nonverbal signs that display readiness to participate
- Listens and follows directions
- Uses appropriate "turn-taking" when communicating with others
- Takes proper turns willingly in activities
- Gives positive feedback and encouragement to others' efforts and success
- Shows acceptance when person doesn't meet one's own expectations
- Is accepting of others who are not successful
- Shows continued effort toward group or individual goals, even if previous attempts were unsuccessful

Level 3:
- Is not always dressed and ready to participate
- May or may not be in assigned space
- Displays inconsistent nonverbal readiness signs
- Interrupts or doesn't listen to others at times
- Demonstrates some trouble waiting for turns
- Is accepting or encouraging to friends' efforts or successes, but not all classmates
- Sometimes demonstrates anger or uncaring attitude toward success attempts
- Continues in activities when successful, gives up when activities are challenging

Level 1:
- Is not physically there and ready to participate (lacks proper equipment, attire, supplies)
- Is roaming within areas outside of expected positions
- Assumes facial/body actions that display lack of readiness to participate
- Determines own course of action
- Talks without regard for others
- Always wants first turn and have most opportunities to participate
- Gives negative verbal feedback ("put-downs")
- Displays negative verbal/nonverbal behaviors when own attempts are unsuccessful
- Displays negative verbal/nonverbal behaviors when others' attempts are not successful
- Gives up and refuses to try after previous group or individual goals were unsuccessful

Figure 7.4 Affective Rubric: Cooperation and Respect in PE (created by M. Wood and S. Phifer).

Rubrics help students and teachers not only determine levels of physical skill but also identify specific behaviors on which to concentrate to improve those skills. The skills could be very general, i.e., how to strike a ball with an object (racket, bat, hockey stick, paddle) so it travels in an intended direction, or designed for a very specific skill, such as the overhand tennis serve, lob, or volley.

Measurement or assessment of attitudes and appreciations tends to be subjective. Clarification of the behaviors that would demonstrate these affective components would define expectations for students. If the objective said, "demonstrate cooperation and respect for self and others," the teacher could ask students to role play some behaviors that would demonstrate the positive and negative aspects of this goal. Students could describe what the behaviors "sounded like" and "looked like"; the teacher could transpose these to a rubric. The teacher might want to post the highest level as an ongoing guide for expected behavior.

USING RUBRICS IN MUSIC CLASSES

Music is another curricular area that may include very broad or very specific outcomes or goals. Elementary music is usually required by all students; objectives include the acquisition of musical skills and appreciations and values. Upper level music classes may have objectives more focused on knowledge or performance of music. Students may also be competing or trying out for roles in singing or instrumental positions. Rubrics could be designed to facilitate the assessment process in any of these situations.

Objectives in the affective domain toward the appreciation and valuing of music are undoubtedly included in music programs across the grade levels. These objectives may be difficult for students to understand and for teachers to evaluate. Rubrics for the objective could be adapted to help all students assess themselves and for teachers to evaluate and teach the expectations for music. The rubrics shown in Figures 7.5, 7.6, 7.7 and 7.8 were developed from the music curriculum of Unified School District No. 489 in Ellis County, Kansas. The objective is to have students develop values of music participation.

Teachers would probably want to share the student self-assessment toward the beginning of the semester, before and after any scheduled

Name: _____

Date: _____ Class: _____

Directions: Think about your own feelings and behaviors about music and music class. Mark in the "yes" box if the statement is true all, or almost all the time. Mark "sometimes" if the statement is true part of the time, and mark "no" if it describes you all or most of the time.

	Yes	Sometimes	No
I like to go to music class.			
I try to do my best when singing and playing musical instruments.			
I take care of the instruments.			
I use best manners and follow directions during programs.			
I make good choices of behavior at program practice.			
I go to, and do my best, at programs.			

Figure 7.5 K–2 *Music Participation Rubric.*

Name: _____

Date: _____ **Class:** _____

Directions: Read each statement and mark the space that best describes your feelings and behaviors during music class and musical practices and performances. Mark "yes" if the statement is true all or most of the time; "no" is seldom and "sometimes" if the statement describes you some of the time.

	Yes	Sometimes	No
I like to go to music class.			
I use a good singing voice.			
I try to play instruments appropriately.			
I handle instruments with care.			
I use proper program behavior.			
I watch and follow the director.			
I make good behavior choices during program practice.			
I attend and participate in programs.			

Goals for Items marked Sometimes or No: Talk with your teacher about items you marked Sometimes or No. Chose one or two; write goals about how you will change your attitudes or behaviors to a Yes; be very specific.

Figure 7.6 Elementary (3–5) Music Values Rubric.

108

Class _____ Date _____

Directions: List students' names down the left column. Check the **Y** for yes if statement describes student's behavior most all the time; **S** for sometimes and **N** for no if student seldom or never displays this behavior.

Behaviors or Attitudes

Student Name	Positive reaction to music	Treats instruments with respect	Shows proper rehearsal techniques	Shows proper rehearsal attitudes	Shows positive performance behaviors

Figure 7.7 Teacher Evaluation Music Appreciation/Attitudes.

Directions: Use the following yes/no rubric in the selection process to determine which candidates will be invited for final tryouts. A more specific rubric might be necessary at that time.

Student's Name: _____   Date: _____

Demonstrated Skill	Yes	No
1. Demonstrates physical clues (eye contact, posture, facial expressions) to self-esteem		
2. Demonstrates diaphragmatic breathing and correct attacks and releases controlled by the breath		
3. Demonstrates correct unison pitch, all major and minor within an octave, perfect intervals, augmented 4th or diminished 5ths		
4. Demonstrates vocal independence when singing part music up to 8-part music		
5. Sight-reads and produces the following intervals: all major and minor 2nds, 3rds, 6ths, 7ths; perfect 4ths, 5ths, unison and octaves, and augmented 4ths and diminished 5ths		
6. Sight-sings simple melody with rhythmic complexities and few accidentals		
7. Sight-sings tonic, dominant, sub-dominant choral harmonies (3-4 part music)		
8. Sight-reads simple 4 part music		
9. Demonstrates rhythmic patterns utilizing combinations of note values and rest values (using recurring pulses of regular and irregular strong and weak beats)		
10. Demonstrates understanding of swing rhythmic notation		
11. Demonstrates dynamic symbols for entire spectrum of musical dynamic and comparative interrelationships		
12. Demonstrates spectrum of art of phrasing (apex) and question and answer (antecedent and consequent) phrasing		

Invited back: Yes   No

Figure 7.8 Music Performance Tryout for Specialty Vocal Group (created by M. Wood and J. Nixon).

performances, and at the conclusion of the semester. Students would then be aware of their expectations and could set goals and assess personal success toward meeting those goals. Music teachers might decide to make an enlarged copy to post as a reminder of expectations and have students show daily progress by the thumbs up, down, or "so-on" nonverbal assessment method.

CONCLUSION

Rubrics are versatile guides that can be constructed to conform to almost any subject matter and for acquisition and demonstration of skills, knowledges, and behaviors in any of the domains. When rubrics are "front-loaded" at the beginning of learning experiences, they act as guides for student expectations during the teaching-learning process and to assess learning outcomes. Teachers can use curriculum objectives as guides to construct rubrics or involve their students in identifying behaviors for the rubrics. When students are involved in all aspects of learning, the probability that they will develop individual responsibility for personal learning behaviors will be greatly enhanced.

8

Student Computer Use and Assessment

Assessment is based on what we believe the child has learned. Instructional technology can be directly involved in various phases of the learning process. It is frequently used to help students learn new material, improve efficiency with already learned material, or produce a product related to the information being learned. It is critically important to understand what instructional technology can do for students in the educational setting as we consider assessment. The expectations we develop for performance are directly related to the purpose of the software we select for our students to use. Software varies greatly in how it can enhance the learning process. These few introductory pages have a great bearing on assessment. They help us understand what the computer can do for our children. It is important that as computer use and assessment is discussed, we have commonality in the terminology we use. If you thoroughly understand categorization and classification of instructional software, you may want to move beyond the first section of this chapter.

CLASSIFICATION OF SOFTWARE

In most classrooms or computer labs today, the computer is used to (1) make something related to an academic task—production, (2) help the students learn facts, figures, names, dates, places, concepts, generalizations, methods, etc.—instruction, (3) program the computer—programming, and (4) glean information—reference.

Production

There are many types of software related to production – word processing, desktop publishing, databases, spreadsheets, paint/draw, calendars, signs, cards, internet, and hypermedia/multimedia. Software that falls into this category is usually quite detailed and requires students to follow specific sequences for the creation of a product. Programs that are relatively new releases or have been recently revised tend to be more intuitive. This means that they are easier to use, and products can eventually be created by most people. It is fairly common for people to say they can use these programs when in fact they might have created only a single product and did that by poking around in the menus without ever looking at the manual to realize the full potential of the program. In fact, they are not efficient, informed, and competent users. The first big hint is to know your software thoroughly. Become a competent and efficient user. The teacher must know the software so he or she can help others learn to be proficient with it. Once the teacher is competent, reasonable tasks can be described using the software.

Instruction

Many companies have created software that focuses on helping our students learn academic material – instruction. Usually we can separate these into four categories: drill and practice, tutorial, simulation, and problem solving. Many of the people who write the documentation for these types of software tell the teacher upfront what they believe their software will do for the student who uses it. The teacher is the one who needs to make the final decision regarding what a piece of software will or will not do for a particular student or group of students.

Drill and practice software assists students to more efficiently use what they have learned. In some situations it is critical in "over learning." One caution that should be offered is that drill and practice software is used after students know something. Drill is used to reinforce material for which there is already a degree of understanding. Teachers have been observed using drill and practice software in an attempt to teach students new facts. Good drill software will be interesting and meaningfully repetitive. It will also have some tutorial sections for immediate error correction, but it will be predominantly drill.

Tutorial software is used by students to learn academic material that the student does not already know. Good tutorial software will contain sections of drill but will be predominantly tutorial. Tutorial software usually takes students through material in definite, small increments with assessment to determine if the knowledge gained is adequate to work efficiently with the topic. If the gain is insufficient, they are usually routed to a place in the software to begin again. If it is sufficient, the user is moved to the next level. There are some major corporations and companies that have specialized in creating huge pieces of tutorial software that are equivalent to courses. These "bigger" pieces of software will frequently involve CD-ROM use and are quite expensive, but definitely have a place in certain learning environments. They are often called by the manufacturer or others Integrated Learning Systems (ILS).

Simulation software models an environment, real or imaginary, in which the user makes decisions that have an important and direct bearing on the final outcome. The software is as good as the model's ability to accurately represent the environment and accept appropriate user input. Students must come to the simulation armed with information. They will be presented with the opportunity to use the information they have and, frequently, a chance to gain some new information. Frequently, students are motivated by the use of simulation software. To the student, it is often game-like in nature, but good simulations are packed with academic information. Simulations are often more complicated, and, therefore, they take longer to learn to use. There are many wonderful simulation pieces of software on the market today.

Problem solving software frequently views good problem solvers as those who possess specific skills used in problem solving and a good understanding of the content that is at the heart of the problem. Much problem-solving software is written to teach or enhance specific skills needed by good problem solvers.

Problem-solving software is actually "content software" like math or reading, but the content happens to be the solving of problems. So this type of software will usually be one of the three types referred to in the previous paragraphs. The teacher must have used the instructional software and feel certain into which category it best fits. Will the students be drilling, learning new information, or interacting in a modeled environment? The teacher can then begin to describe the student behaviors to be expected because of student use.

All these forms of instructional software vary greatly with how much teacher input is available to alter the content, and they also vary regarding the teacher's ability to gain information. For example, some drill software would allow the teacher to modify the software so the students could work with a specific set of words, examples, and definitions. Others would require the piece of software as it was manufactured. Some software can, therefore, be more closely aligned with a specific set of standards, performances, goals, or objectives.

Programming

When most people hear about programming, they imagine an adult computer scientist or some wonder child. In fact, many elementary schools teach a computer language—LOGO. This language was designed specifically for children so they could make the computer do what they told it to do. Many middle schools now offer literacy courses in which students are exposed to Basic computer language. Of course, most high schools afford students the opportunity to learn Basic, Pascal, or C either in a class with that as the specific goal or in a math- or science-related course where the computer language is used as a tool. Usually, the language is learned and used to cause the computer to help humans solve problems. Every type of software referred to in the previous paragraphs is written in some type of computer language.

Reference

Computer software used as a reference source includes many different types of encyclopedias and specific database collections, which are mostly contained on a CD-ROM. It is accessed by the computer. Another reference source that is growing in popularity is the internet. The computer or the computer network accesses the internet using special software. The internet is actually a huge number of computers, each with a specific address. These computers may be visited, and the information on the computers can be viewed and transferred to the user's computer. The individual or school gains access to the internet by means of an internet provider. This access is provided for a fee. The internet holds a wealth of information. One drawback from a teacher's point of view is that it is uncensored.

In Conclusion

For students who are learning software, teachers frequently make "reminder" sheets. This helps them with confusing or complex sections of the software. It is also common to see teachers modeling the use of the software for their students. Though overall software is getting easier to use, it is sometimes difficult to make decisions about exactly what would be the best thing to do next, where to locate specific menu choices, or how to deal with a menu choice once selected. After the students have used the software for a while, they should not need to refer to the reminder sheets unless they are very young users or the process is quite intricate and cumbersome. A good rule of thumb is that if you, the experienced older person, are confused, the student will most likely have similar problems. This does not necessarily work the other way around. Just because the teacher can breeze through the software without confusion does not mean the students' experiences will be the same. The teacher always needs to be the "devil's advocate" when determining how students will function with the software.

Finally, teachers need the following computer literacy skills to use computers effectively in the classroom. Know what you want your students to accomplish, locate the potential software, and read the documentation. Learn to use it thoroughly as though you were the student. Determine what type of help students will need to learn the software. Then, you are closer to starting academic computing with your students.

ASSESSMENT OF STUDENTS USING ACADEMIC SOFTWARE

All faculty make decisions every day regarding the quality and/or quantity of student work and whether or not it is up to standard. The accuracy of these decisions varies greatly. These pages are intended to assist the instructor in developing and using a more authentic system of assessment. The following is Becky's story of how she developed assessment instruments needed for an internet project she initiated. Becky is really a collection of many teachers I have seen over the years who have developed internet activities. There are many cautions any teacher would want to be aware of when taking students onto the internet for academic purposes. Most school districts have internet use policies. In these policies, student, parent, faculty, and administration rights and responsibilities regarding internet use are specifically explained.

Becky's Story

Becky just purchased internet services for her home computer through a local internet provider about a month ago. She has explored every place imaginable. Tile, topics, and information keep popping up that are related to what her students are learning in class. This internet neophyte/teacher is beginning to grasp the idea that her students would benefit from time using the internet. She knows she is starting to feel quite comfortable finding her way around the internet, but she wonders if she is using the same skills a student would use when searching and retrieving data related to a class project. Becky is bothered by what she is sure her school would deem as unfit material for a public school setting, such as pornography, violence, and drugs. Right now, when she makes an assignment, students do not sift through or reference "unfit" material, but she sees that as a potential problem with internet access by her students. She still believes this resource to be too great to leave untapped by her students.

Thinking like an educator, she decides to approach this issue "backwards." Educators frequently decide what result they want before considering how they will arrive at that end. First, meaning last, what should the students have when they are finished? This teacher envisions a two-page, word-processed paper constructed entirely from facts gleaned from the internet. The paper will contain a special reference section, which will list all the addresses of the internet sites used in the paper. These addresses will be numbered, and these numbers will be used as bibliographical references.

Still thinking in reverse, she questions, "What did they have to do to get there?" "What skills will they have to have in place?" To herself, she declares, "let's save a tree or two" – my students will electronically transfer notes from the internet to the word processor, then they will word process the *paper* from their notes. They will turn in a floppy disk with their notes and the *paper* saved on it. She believes they can find key articles on the internet, then in a word processor record the address of where the information was found, then copy selected internet information from that address into that file. That file will be used as notes to later write the *paper.*

Becky now sees three areas of concern for her project: 1) student word processing, 2) searching the internet and retrieving appropriate data, and 3) switching back and forth between the internet search engine and the word processor. With a little bit of worry, she ponders, "besides having a coherent paper as I normally require, I have opened up three more areas that need to be assessed." She makes notes in her planning notebook that by assessing these three areas, it would act as formative assessment and help the students along the way to successful completion of the overall project. Becky then recorded the following rough outline, which she believes would later help her design assessment devices.

I. Internet
  A. Finding and opening internet program
  B. Changing the search engine
  C. Creating and entering proper words for the search
  D. Recognizing and selecting appropriate articles from the title and abstract
  E. Getting to the site
  F. Book marking the site
  G. Highlighting a portion of text at a sight
  H. Copying to memory the highlighted portion of the internet article

II. Word Processing
  A. Finding and opening the word processor (wp) program
  B. Creating a new wp document/Opening an already existing wp document
  C. Moving from one open file to another
  D. Typing and error correction in a wp document
  E. Spell checking a wp document
  F. Saving a document to a student-owned floppy disk
  G. Pasting text into a wp document that was copied from another document

III. Switching Programs
  A. Being at an internet site and moving to the wp without shutting down either
  B. Being in the wp and moving to an internet site without shutting down either

She began to muse, "Seems like either they could do those things in the outline or they couldn't." Then it occurred to her, as she reflected on her own beginnings, "When I first started, I could muddle through poking here and there until I finally found the right menu items to use and finally figured out what to do—so for my students, I will make part of the assessment a proficiency or efficiency rating." Though she does not consider herself an expert on "teaching others software," she does know that with meaningful repetition and corrective feedback or formative assessment, students become more proficient with the task. With this in mind, she decides to develop tasks related to the required aspects of the internet project. She knows that it will be a reasonable expectation to have her students open programs, find, and then use menu items in an efficient manner. After several smaller assignments, each focusing on a portion of the overall project, she can imagine her students clicking, dragging, highlighting, copying, pasting, writing, and keyboarding their way smoothly through the final assignment.

Becky's first attempt at an assessment instrument for the word processing portions of the assignment looked like those in Figure 8.1. She was not pleased. The descriptors in the header did not apply to all assessment items equally well. She created the assessment in Figure 8.2.

Becky was much more pleased with her second attempt. She was especially pleased with the fact that each level contained the same number and type of descriptors. She realized some of her students

Internet	Quickly/Efficiently	With Deliberation and/or some Errors	Slowly and/or Several Errors
finds program icon			
changes search engine			
enters search words			
search words are appropriate			
book marks site			
highlights selected text			
copies highlighted text			

Figure 8.1 Internet (first attempt) Rubric.

Level 5 - Internet skills efficiently executed
_____finds and opens internet program *without* hesitation or delay
_____changes from Yahoo(default) to Web Crawler (desired) *without* hesitation or delay
_____selects fewest words to appropriately do search
_____makes no spelling errors
_____records 3 of 3 article titles resulting from search that are closely related to topic
_____records 3 of 3 article titles resulting from search definitely not related to topic
_____reviews only academically-related sites and does so quickly
_____selects only the necessary menu items to book mark a site
_____book marks an academically related site from the search
_____highlights an important section of text suitable for notes, but not all the text
_____executes the copy feature on the first attempt and does so quickly

Level 3 - Internet skills are acceptable
_____finds and opens internet program *with* hesitation or delay
_____changes from Yahoo (default) to Web Crawler (desired) *with* hesitation or delay
_____does not use fewest words to appropriately do search, but it works
_____makes text free of spelling errors in search words
_____2 of 3 article titles indicated as closely related are
_____2 of 3 article titles indicated as not related are not
_____reviews academically-related sites slowly; with hesitation
_____makes some unnecessary choices when looking for menu items to book mark a site
_____has difficulty figuring out how to book mark a related site from the search
_____has difficulty highlighting a specific section of text, but eventually does so
_____takes more than one attempt to copy text or does so quite slowly

Level 1 - Internet skills needs more work
_____has difficulty locating internet program, requires some assistance
_____has great difficulty changing from Yahoo to Web Crawler
_____use of search topic wording is inappropriate or off target
_____has spelling errors
_____1 of 3 article titles resulting from search indicated as closely related are
_____1 of 3 article titles resulting from search indicated as not related are not
_____reviews non-academically related site(s)
_____selects only the necessary menu items to book mark a site
_____lacks understanding of book marking functions
_____has difficulty highlighting a specific section of text, requires assistance
_____copied text is done by apparent trial and error

Figure 8.2 Internet (second attempt) Rubric.

would end up on the border and receive 2s and 4s, but that is okay with a rubric.

When the big day came and she was ready to begin the project, she explained the project, discussed each item or each instrument with her classes and explained why each item appeared on an assessment. Becky's assessment instrument for word processing appears in Figure 8.3, and the assessment instrument for switching programs appears in Figure 8.4.

One thing with which Becky would agree at this point is the saying, "Success is a journey not a destination." We should probably modify

Level 5 -Word Processing - <u>Excellent</u> - <u>Efficient</u>
_____has difficulty locating internet program, requires some assistance
_____creates new wp documents without hesitation, delay or wrong menu choices
_____changes directory from "C" drive to "A" drive when opening files without hesitation
_____opens already existing files that are on the "A" drive (student floppy)
_____moves back and forth between two open wp files at the same time, quickly
_____spells and corrects words efficiently
_____replaces entire word and/or sentences using highlight & type
_____locates the spelling checker without hesitation
_____uses the spelling checker easily and quickly
_____pastes words or sentences copied from another document into a wp
        document quickly

Level 3 - Word Processing - <u>Acceptable</u>
_____finds and opens word processing program with hesitation or delay
_____creates new wp documents with hesitation, delay
_____changes directory from "C" drive to "A" drive when opening files but slow and
        methodically
_____opens already existing files that are on the "A" drive (student floppy) but slow
        and unsure about procedure
_____moves back and forth between two open wp files on second main menu item guess
_____corrects spelling and typing errors; but hesitant in the process
_____replaces entire word and/or sentences using delete or back space key; is hesitant in
        actions
_____locates the spelling checker on second guess
_____uses the spelling checker, but appears to be hesitant and concerned
_____pastes word or sentence copied from another document into a wp
        document; requires some menu trial and error

Level 1 - Word Processing Skills - <u>Needs More Work</u>
_____finds and opens internet program with much hesitation, delay, & guessing
_____creates new wp documents, but with hesitation, delay and wrong menu choices
_____has great difficulty changing drives from "C" drive to "A" drive when opening files
        appears unsure and may requires several attempts or choices
_____opens already existing files that are on the "A" drive (student floppy)
_____moves back and forth between two wp files open at the same time, but requires
        much time and or several guesses
_____corrects spelling of words but has difficulty, apparent guessing about function
        of keys
_____replaces entire words and/or sentences; process is guess-filled and awkward
_____locates the spelling checker given many guesses
_____lacks clear understanding of how all spelling checker functions work
_____pastes word or sentence copied from another document into a wp
        document, but it may end up any place and requires menu trial and error

Figure 8.3 Word Processing Rubric.

that saying to read, "The creation of a successful assessment instrument is a journey," because assessment is truly a process. Looking back at Becky's process, she did a lot of thinking before she ever wrote anything down, but when she did her first writing, she did not consider it a final copy simply because it was written. She went from an outline to an unusable instrument to what she considered a usable instrument. She went from telling the story in her mind of the desired student behaviors to writing them down. The writing process often forces us to look much more critically at what has been roaming around in our minds. On paper, it requires much more substance and structure. Telling a story of expected student behaviors in an important step in the process of assessment development. Very few of us can just "think things through," then create a final product.

Becky was obviously a user of the software she was expecting her students to use. A second situation is quite different from Becky's story. In this situation, the students will be using simulation software – a type of instructional software. The students will also be working at computers in teams of four or cooperative small groups. Though this situation is very different from students surfing the internet and writing papers, the preparation for assessment has many general similarities. The teacher still has to ask, "Why am I assessing?" and "What form should it take?" The teacher has to be exceptionally familiar with the software and how it can be used by a small group. Many years ago, I heard an educator say that teaching was as easy as pie. What this person meant was that teaching was as Planning Implementing Evaluating. Whether or not instruction involves modern instructional technology, these are still essential components of good teaching/learning. The words used to describe these components have changed over time, but the educator still must prepare himself or herself and the students. Action must be taken on plans, and then in some formative and/or summative way

Level 5 -Switching Between Word Processing and Internet Programs - Excellent - Efficient

_____ knows which button on the menu bar is the minimize button
_____uses the minimize button on the menu bar in the transition process
_____uses the task bar icon related to the program to which they wish to switch
_____performs entire switching process smoothly and quickly with no wrong choices

Level 3 - Switching Between Word Processing and Internet Programs - Acceptable

_____ confuses which buttons on the menu bar perform which functions
_____switches programs by closing and opening programs
_____ is slow with switching process, but is eventually completed; not efficient

Level 1 - Switching Between Word Processing and Internet Programs - Needs More Work

_____ is confused about which buttons on the menu bar perform which functions
_____accomplishes transition only by closing and opening programs, with
        some assistance from another
_____is slow with entire switching process; not efficient, data may be lost

Figure 8.4 *Rubric for Checking Student's Ability to Switch Programs.*

assessment will happen. Having been a student of cooperative learning, Jean decided to combine cooperative learning and students using a computer simulation.

Jean's Students Work Cooperatively on a Computer Simulation

Jean was a science teacher and located a piece of software that met several of the objectives she wanted her students to meet, and it gave them the chance to practice some performances that were part of the standards for her science department as well as the state. Her students were going to be learning more about, as well as enhancing, their ability to use some science process skills. They would accomplish this through good classroom instruction coupled with the group use of a simulation program. One area of assessment of interest to Jean was the ability to function cooperatively while sharing one computer and one piece of software. This assessment was going to be formative in nature. The students were going to be observed as they worked at the computer, and there would be some type of debriefing on a daily basis. The students would spend about four class periods working with the simulation. Jean expected great things and was at least pleased with the outcome. All students were told they would be assessed on the cooperative nature of their group (Figure 8.5). This form of assessment as defined by Taggart and Wood earlier in this text would probably be analytic. The items they were told the assessor would be listening and watching for as they worked as a group were use of roles, sharing talking time, using first names, discussing issues, business-like noise level in group, polite language, and teamwork. Individually, they would be observed for efficient time use, polite language, maintaining private records, and being responsible for their own learning. One might ask, "What does any of that have to do with using computers in instruction?" The response would have to be that the environment in which learning takes place is critically important to the quality of learning. The atmosphere in the computer lab where students are supposed to be concentrating on the information being presented by the software is important. Jean was assessing the behavior of students as they used the software. She already had a high degree of confidence in their ability to operate the software and make decisions affecting the outcome of the simulation.

Level 5: High Level Group Behaviors

Group members

_____maintain their role and expected others to stay in theirs
_____wait to talk, concisely make their point, non-verbally recognize others to speak
_____use first names in both questions and response with others all the time
_____disagree agreeably, "attitude" was missing, language was factual
_____use business-like voice level in group
_____use polite language; students complimented and encouraged each other
_____share work load willingly; exemplified team work

Level 3: Mid-Level Group Behaviors

Group members

_____maintain their role most of the time
_____take turns talking
_____frequently use first names when asking question <u>or</u> when giving a response
_____disagree agreeably most of the time; but opinions and attitudes
       occasionally got in the way and prevented calm collected discourse, "attitudes"
       were sometimes noticeable
_____often use business-like voice level; sometimes social noise prevailed
_____occasionally use compliments and encouragement; some impolite language is evident
_____team work is occasionally noticeable - work load was often shared willingly

Level 1: Low Level Group Behaviors

Group members

_____have a difficult time maintaining their roles
_____ sometimes take turns talking, but talk over others frequently
_____ use first names infrequently — students frequently just start talking,
       conversation often is not specifically directed
_____allow opinions and attitudes to get in the way and prevent the group from having an
       atmosphere of positive exchange
_____use voice level which is not business-like, social noise prevails
_____use impolite language, students seldom use compliments and encouragement
_____seldom work as a team - work load is not shared willingly

Figure 8.5 Rubric for Assessing Group Use of Computer Simulations.

LOGO Programming Language

Many elementary teachers in the United States are introducing their students to LOGO programming. Teachers are interested in helping the students develop better problem-solving skills, as well as an understanding of what programming is like. One of the most popular areas of LOGO is a graphic section. In the graphic area, the cursor is called a turtle, and the students type in commands that make the turtle obey. The turtle responds to the wishes of the student. A turtle command consists of a word or abbreviation sometimes followed by a number. The beginning commands that need to be learned first are called primitive commands. When the turtle moves across the screen, it usually leaves behind a line. The student can learn to create designs by having the turtle travel a specific course. By moving forward and turning a specific number of degrees then going forward and turning again and on and on, the student can create boxes, hexagons, etc. This is a list of the primitive commands.

Command	Abbreviation	Function
clear graphics	CG	clear the screen
forward	FD 25	move turtle forward
back	BK 18	moves turtle backward
right	RT 45	rotates turtle degrees right
left	LT 270	rotates turtle degrees left
pen up	PU	turtle moves without leaving a line behind where it went
pen down	PD	turtle moves leaving a line
home	HOME	turtle returns to center of grid
hide turtle	HT	cursor disappears, but it can still leave a line behind
show turtle	ST	makes cursor reappear

Children learn this language by using it. Normally, the instruction would begin by introducing a command then allowing the student to practice using the command. Next, the teacher would pose a problem for the students to solve by using the command they have just learned. Students may be expected to use commands that were learned in any previous lesson. For example, if students previously learned the FD # command, they know they must have a space between the letters and the number, and they also know the larger the number, the farther the turtle will move. If today the RT # command is introduced, the students will learn that the turtle will spin or rotate on an axis. They will learn that they can make the turtle face backward by commanding RT 180 or they can make the turtle turn to the right by commanding RT 90. They will also learn that the turtle has its own right and left. So if the turtle's nose is pointing up the screen, the turtle's right is the student's right, but if the turtle's nose is pointing down, then his right is the student's left. The problem-solving challenge offered by the teacher may seem simple, but for young, first-time LOGO programmers, it will be a challenge. The teacher poses this problem: using as few commands as pos-

In the construction of a rectangle after introduction and practice with the LOGO command RT # and FD #, the student will be able to answer yes to the following questions.

yes	no	I did not have to clear graphic (CG) and start over
yes	no	I only used the logo commands RT and FD
yes	no	Each time I entered the **RT** command I followed it with a space and a number
yes	no	Each time I entered the **FD** command I followed it with a space and a number
yes	no	Each time I enter the RT command I used 90 as the number
yes	no	I create a rectangle (2 long sides & 2 short sides)-- not a box
yes	no	The two long sides were the same length
yes	no	The two short sides were the same length
yes	no	I was able to make a rectangle and enter only 7 commands

Figure 8.6 Logo Programming for Primary Grades.

sible, make the turtle leave a trail behind him that will be shaped like a rectangle. Because some students begin learning LOGO before they begin their formal keyboarding (grade 3 or 4), the students are not being judged on keyboard entry, rather they are being observed to see how well they have retained the information about the syntax and their ability to logically command the turtle. The rubric used to assess their performance would be relatively simple. The keyboard command they enter would be like these but probably with different numeric values – FD25 RT90 FD40 RT90 FD25 RT90 FD40. A rubric used to assess this LOGO programming appears in Figure 8.6.

Rubric construction and use when dealing with technology, whether it be computers or calculators, is warranted. When teachers take the time to think through the criteria and the process they want their students to understand, student expectations are kept in a meaningful perspective, and the true outcome of the experience may be assessed. Rubrics provide teachers with the flexible tool they need to assess the types of performance tasks to which technology yields itself. An added bonus is experienced when rubrics are used in the affective domain, such as the cooperative learning experience chronicled in this chapter.

The Diverse Learner: Setting Meaningful Criteria

INTRODUCTION

In classrooms across the world, teachers work with students of varied abilities, cultures, and experiences. These factors may attribute to a spread of at least two to three grade levels within a class regardless of age. This writer's definition of special learners is broad and encompasses a large range of educational needs.

Special learners are students who may need extra adult help, varied learning experiences, learning aids, alternative assessments, and more time to acquire goals and objectives that meet minimum grade level expectations. They may be at, above, or below grade level working toward a developmental progression of selected skills necessary to live and work in society. They all have a need for teacher intervention and individual planning to meet specific educational goals.

There are students who fall between the cracks and are not on individual education plans who are still considered at-risk special learners. Students who are learning English as a second language also have special needs. Rubrics are helpful in establishing where students are on a continuum of skills to be acquired.

LEARNING FACTORS

Teaching experience indicates the following factors have significant effect on the learning of all students.

- language development (foundation of learning): (1) receptive and expressive language experiences, (2) ability to understand

directions, and (3) ability to listen, follow, and carry out directions
- culture/family expectations
- school expectations
- emotional and physical health
- attention span
- social skills
- peer groups in class and outside of class
- attitude, self-control, and ability to follow the rules
- retention of learned experiences
- teacher attitude, education, and experience

Many factors affect the learning process. There is constant research for new methods of assessment and teaching strategies that may be implemented to meet the needs of all students. The above factors are those that seem to arise on a continuing basis when students are experiencing difficulty in learning. These factors are included in the rubrics displayed, as they are detrimental to the learning continuum.

Language is the basis of all learning. From the very beginning of life, infants learn to associate sounds, images, tastes, touches, and smells to certain objects or people. They will actively explore their environment using all the sensorimotor modalities to learn cause and effect relationships. Language and problem solving go hand in hand. Infants will exhibit purposeful, goal-directed movement to solve basic needs problems. They will crawl toward an interesting object or special person, vocalize for food or attention, and cry when hungry, hurt, or lonely. Infants learn to label their environment with consistent sounds they hear associated with particular input from caregivers. Infants will search out someone with whom to communicate on a very basic level of eye contact and random vocalizations.

As infants mature, language matures into many gestures and a wide variety of vocalizations. Nouns and verbs are used; however, speech may be unintelligible to the nonfamiliar listener. Simple cause and effect responses such as pushing the TV button and watching the TV picture appear are understood. Phrases are understood, and attention to adult conversation is lengthened as more and more language makes sense connecting people, objects, needs, wants, and activities with what is important to the child.

By the time children enter kindergarten, their language usually contains a wide variety of vocabulary words. Adult attention and response to a student's questions are important. Students not only communicate needs, wants, and ideas to their teachers, but also peers and other adults in the school setting. A few articulation errors may be present. The students continue to perfect questioning skills to gain new information.

Students who have a deficient language base, a breakdown in language, or a different language spoken at home than is spoken at school are at risk for learning problems. Students labeled Learning Disabled, At-Risk, ESL, Learning Challenged, Mentally Disabled, Autistic, Speech and Language Disorder, etc., all experience a breakdown in language development. Social and behavioral problems often result from inability to communicate.

It is extremely difficult when students are placed in situations where their native (already learned) language is not used and they are expected to learn a new set of symbols to communicate. Words learned most quickly are those necessary for survival and comfort (hungry, eat, drink, bathroom, food item requests, help family members, etc.). Favorite toys, activities, places, people, and items used in everyday living are some of the first words needed in a new language. Eye contact will vary depending on the culture, but visuals and tangible objects are helpful and necessary for new language acquisition.

For better understanding of the difficulties experienced by ESL students, consider an adult traveling to another country where English is not spoken. He or she would have to learn words and phrases like, "I need help. Where can we eat? Where is the bathroom? What is your name? My name is _____." The traveler also needs to know the official greeting of the culture. Even within a culture, there are innately learned rules for language. For example, high school students may say "Eh" or "Yo" in response to peers' greetings. However, this would not be an acceptable greeting in job interviews. Students going to school where another language is spoken have to learn a new set of rules for the language in addition to learning the unique language and culture of a particular school. One of the first skills students learn is how to communicate with surrounding adults and classmates in an appropriate and acceptable manner. This can be the nonverbal use of eye contact, gestures, and hand signs. Being noticed and accepted as part of the social group is vital and depends on teacher intervention with peer groupings and class activities to promote acceptance and understanding of someone who has special needs. Teacher attitude and intervention can make a significant difference in how the class accepts someone and includes him or her in their learning family.

It is vital for teachers to learn the important factors in the lives of students who speak another language or have language difficulties. It is helpful to learn family names and structures, pet names, food preferences, special toys, books, activities, and especially fears students may have. For students experiencing difficulty understanding and communicating, anything familiar and special will increase confidence and motivation to attempt new learning.

Teachers need to be certain students with language problems are in close proximity and are given various modes of instruction in addition to verbal directions. Pictures, modeling, and acting out situations or specific actions all help receptive language development. Extra time, attention, and reinforcement are needed to help these students move toward appropriate expressive language.

Reading, writing, math, science, and social studies all incorporate language that is heard, spoken, understood, questioned, and formulated with opinions and facts. Music, art, and physical education are sometimes a haven for students who have language difficulties, providing expectations are appropriate. Even these disciplines incorporate unique language all their own. Especially helpful are visual and auditory models when they are consistently provided with verbal directions.

ASSESSING LANGUAGE DEVELOPMENT

The Language Rubric in Figure 9.1 may be useful, but needs to be open to continued revision and input from language specialists and ESL teachers. The rubric is an outgrowth of teaching experience, professional development, and professional reading.

For students to reach the level of fluency in the language rubric, they must make progress as described using the Dependency Levels Rubric. Two Dependency Level Rubrics are described. The Dependency Level Rubric was developed in 1985 by Ryabik and Webster at an early childhood developmental center. The term "rubric" was not used; instead, it was simply called Dependency Levels. Children's goals and objectives were written using the dependency level model. The model was used for children with disabilities and typically developing children.

Readiness: The Student -
- Develops a language base for connecting symbols to specific needs, people, places, and things.
- Expresses needs and wants using body language, words and vocalizations understandable to immediate caregivers.
- Understands simple directions and responds appropriately.
- Matches main words to the pictures seen and can sit through a short story.
- May need adult assistance to clarify meaning in certain situations.

Emergent: Student -
- Pairs words with objects, people or events and relates important recent experiences.
- Answers simple questions and asks similar who, what, and where questions.
- Continues to expand and improve vocabulary. Sentences become longer (five to ten words).
- Communicates mainly to immediate family, caregivers and close friends.
- Is understandable to familiar adults but does not always use pronouns and verbs appropriately.

Developing: Student -
- Communicates wants and needs to a variety of care givers and adults in structured and nonstructured settings.
- Explains important events using three to six sentences or more.
- Makes inferences from language and explains specific situations.
- Takes turns talking and listening during group discussion.
- Maintains eye contact with the listener and/or speaker and doesn't talk while others are talking.
- Is understandable to most adults and peers.

Fluent: Student -
- Asks and answers subjective (who, what, where, how, when, why) questions related to personal and school situations.
- Initiates and participates in communication with a variety of adults in various settings.
- States opinions and beliefs related to the social behaviors of others.
- Shows an awareness of environmental and current social issues by stating likes and dislikes.
- States and supports opinions and beliefs.

Figure 9.1 Assessing Language Development Rubric.

Dependency Levels reflect the way the learner manages himself/herself in the preschool environment. It does not necessarily correspond to stages of development. A learner with a physical disability who is unable to verbally communicate may be called semi-independent due to the ability to complete a task on his/her own developmental level.

Dependent: Adult is in very close proximity and gives much verbal prompting and reinforcement. Physical manipulation may be necessary.

1. Does not follow the routine, although she/he may know the routine.
2. May physically resist task initiation and completion.
3. May initiate and complete some tasks, but not others.

Semi-Dependent: Adult can send to do a task but should monitor at least every minute. Some verbal prompting is necessary and much reinforcement should be given.

1. Knows routine, but does not always follow it without adult prompting.
2. May complete tasks without prompting if adult is within visual field.

Semi-Independent: Adult can send to do a task but should monitor every 3-5 minutes. Very little verbal prompting is necessary and much reinforcement should be given.

1. Knows routine and can follow it, but may be distracted by other children or activities.
2. Will perform structured group activities with teacher in view.

Independent: Can complete tasks independently, but much reinforcement should be given.

1. Knows routine and will initiate and complete tasks with little or no prompting.
2. Will perform structured group activities even though teacher may not be in view.

Figure 9.2 Dependency Levels Rubric (from Ryabik and Webster, 1985).

Dependency Levels reflect the way the learner manages himself/herself in the classroom. It does not necessarily correspond to chronological age, IQ, or stages of development. It reflects student work habits, self-control, and ability to initiate and complete various tasks independently.

Dependent: Adult is in very close proximity to student and gives much verbal prompting, redirection and reinforcement to complete tasks. Directions may need to be restated several times.

1. Does not follow the routine, although she/he may know the routine
   Student may forget the routine or not even be aware of it.
2. May resist task initiation and completion; waits/watches for
   adult to begin or continue work.
3. May initiate and complete some tasks and not others, or may
   initiate but not complete tasks without adult direction.
4. Adult is responsible for child completing tasks.

Semi-Dependent: Adult can send student to work on a task but monitors every three to five minutes. Some verbal prompting is necessary and much reinforcement is given.

1. Knows routine, but does not always follow it without adult
   prompting/direction.
2. May complete tasks without prompting if adult is within visual field.
3. Takes some responsibility for learning but needs adult prompting to
   continue working and stay on task.

Semi-Independent: Adult can send student to work on a task but should monitor every five to ten minutes. Little verbal prompting is necessary and moderate, intermittent reinforcement is given.

1. Knows routine and can follow it, but may be distracted by other
   children or activities.
2. Performs structured group and individual work activities with teacher in
   view.
3. Takes more responsibility for learning but still needs adult approval and
   guidelines.

Independent: Child can complete tasks independently; wants adult approval, but is proud of own work and confident to initiate and share own ideas.

1. Knows routine and initiates and complete tasks with little or no
   prompting.
2. Performs activities and completes work with teacher not in view.

Figure 9.3 Dependency Rubric.

The developmental center was a special purpose infant–toddler early intervention program and preschool with an enrollment of two-thirds students with disabilities and one-third typically developing students. The inclusion model and peer teaching methods were used at this center before they were popular names and trends in education. Even though the developmental levels were written for children from birth through preschool age, they are easily adaptable for use at all levels.

The original Dependency Levels developed by Ryabik and Webster

(1985) are shown in Figure 9.2. The second Dependency Rubric is an adaptation that is presented as Figure 9.3.

CONCLUSION

In summary, the language and dependency rubrics displayed in this chapter can be used by classroom teachers to assess present levels of student abilities and help them plan for specific learning goals. Language and dependency levels are two basic ideas that significantly affect learning. If a child is having learning problems, one or both of these areas is usually involved. Rubrics are not meant to create more paperwork or be another checklist to complete. Rather, they are to be used as effective tools to plan for productive learning. The rubrics displayed in this chapter are not perfect or totally finished. They will be under constant revision as they are used by a variety of teachers with diverse groups of students. Readers are encouraged to adapt rubrics as needed and utilize them to improve learning goals in their classrooms.

REFERENCE

Ryabik, D. and T. Webster. 1985. *Early Childhood Developmental Curriculum.* Hays, Kansas: unpublished.

Rubrics: A Tool for Ongoing Teacher Evaluation

A HISTORICAL LOOK AT TEACHER EVALUATION

Teacher effectiveness has been continuously investigated in the past decade since instructional improvement was prompted by such calls as *A Nation at Risk* (National Commission on Excellence in Education, 1983) and *High School: A Report on Secondary Education in America* (Boyer, 1983). These studies investigate relationships between specific teacher behavior and student achievement. Recommendations for improvement run the gamut from higher expectations for both teachers and students to smaller class size to more active involvement on the part of students with teachers taking a facilitative role.

Effectiveness deals both with technical skill and opportunities to exercise that skill. Principals are the school leaders most often responsible for the evaluation of teaching effectiveness at both levels. They must have a sense of the culture of the school, research on effective strategies, and a sense of planning so that determinations can be made to benefit instruction. Such a sense takes many forms. The Teacher Education Conference Board of New York (1981) offers a list of ten important educator characteristics. Educators must

- stay current with professional knowledge and skill
- continue to be involved in intellectual activity
- be aware of social expectations, institutional goals, and professional responsibilities
- be open-minded to advances in pedagogical practices
- become proficient in planning and implementation of objectives
- manage and perform instructional functions effectively

- have concern for students as individuals
- be a dependable member of the staff
- be dedicated
- contribute talents to community welfare and improvement

Adler (1982) limited his vision of teaching effectiveness to possessing three attributes: didactive instruction, coaching, and Socratic questioning. Wlodkowski (1985) identifies four essential teacher qualities: expertise, empathy, enthusiasm, and clarity, adding that teachers must be able to make the learning experience meaningful and enjoyable.

Purkey and Novak (1984) developed three major skill areas: being ready, being with, and following through. Being ready includes the efforts of the teacher to provide a safe, clean, and comfortable learning environment. Being with invites teachers to reach each student, develop a trusting relationship, be able to read situations, make situations inviting, communicate clearly, provide choices, and handle student rejection. Following through occurs when desired results are not produced. The teacher examines possibilities for that failure and initiates strategies to increase the probability of success.

Additional models include Hunter's clinical teaching, which involved teachers as decision makers and use of research-based data on factors affecting student learning, which can help teachers make sound instructional decisions. A model by Bloom stresses teaching for mastery with teacher traits involving four key elements: cues, reinforcements, feedback and correctives, and student engagement.

To say that one approach to teaching effectively is preferable or that one set of teacher characteristics allows for better student achievement is not the point of this section. Numerous models exist when discussing teaching effectiveness. The key becomes the development of a district model that is eclectic, fitting the nature of the school and the needs of the learning community. Proponents of such an integration often include the following six situations: planning, classroom management, instruction, monitoring of progress, clinical assistance, and care of students. The success of schools is dependent upon consensus by the school community on the meaning and parameters of each situation. The principal, as instructional leader, is responsible for aiding the staff in reaching consensus. One means for doing this is by collaboratively setting parameters that indicate criteria for success in each area prior to the commencement of the school year.

LINKING TEACHING EFFECTIVENESS TO TEACHER EVALUATION

"Evaluations of educators should promote sound education principles, fulfillment of institutional missions, and effective performance of job responsibilities, so that the educational needs of students, community, and society are met" (The Joint Committee on Standards for Educational Evaluation, 1988, p. 21). Thus, the link to teaching effectiveness is obvious.

The most critical situations instructional leaders must deal with is the supervision and development of teachers. It is in this context that improvement toward teaching effectiveness is most likely to occur. Supervision entails knowledge of what it takes to be an effective teacher: direct monitoring of instruction and collection of data that may be used in setting goals for improvement. You will see that this is not very different from the role of the teacher. A teacher starts with sound content and pedagogical knowledge, monitors progress of instruction and learning, then uses the data collected or the reflections made to set or adjust teaching or learning goals.

While many educators express a desire to separate supervision from evaluation of teachers, current time constraints, laws, and administrative practices make this highly unlikely. Evaluation is defined as a formal process by which judgments are made about the extent to which desired outcomes have been achieved. Summative evaluations represent a final accountability, often affecting a person's employment status, while formative evaluation is an interim judgment intended to provide developmental information to the person being evaluated. Formative and summative evaluations are at times in conflict. Formative evaluation is often used in conjunction with supervision, which requires a bond of trust between teacher and evaluator. Summative evaluation, emphasizing judgment, puts that trusting relationship at risk.

Several educators have proposed standards for evaluation. Darling-Hammond, Wise, and Pease (1983) suggest four minimal conditions for the operation of teacher evaluation systems:

- shared understanding of the criteria and processes for teacher evaluation
- shared understanding of how criteria and process relate to important aspects of teaching

- shared perception that evaluation enables and motivates teachers to improve performance
- shared perception of a balance between control and autonomy

Duke (1987) adds five essential structural components that must be in place in workable evaluation systems:

- vision of teaching or set of performance standards
- procedures for collecting high-quality data on teaching performance
- mechanisms for delivering useful feedback
- resources for helping teachers improve their performance
- procedures for handling inadequate teacher performance

Duke adds that performance standards must be clearly written, based on current research, developed as a result of teacher input, and are widely publicized and reviewed regularly. The standards should also be linked to the teacher job description. Stiggins and Bridgeford (1985) further suggest that instructional skills be the focus of the standards and that inferences be minimized.

TEACHER/PRINCIPAL-CREATED RUBRICS: WHY AND HOW?

Care must be exercised in creating instruments to be used in evaluation. Validity can be achieved by involving teachers in the development of evaluation instruments, by establishing the criteria on which they will be judged, and by providing staff development to help teachers learn behaviors that meet the specified criteria. Reliability refers to consistency in ratings of the same teacher by different evaluators and whether an individual evaluator is consistent in ratings over time. Training of evaluators is necessary to ensure reliability. Evaluation instruments should be tested to ensure that they do not discriminate against individuals or groups, or produce different results when applied to varied teaching situations such as subject matter, class size, or type of student (Smith, Peterson, and Micceri, 1987).

Rubrics are used as an evaluation tool. By using a rubric, the evaluator assesses the quality of instruction using a numerical rating. The rubric created by the teacher and evaluator, or entire faculty and evaluator, provides a format for review of the teaching process. It allows for the teacher to think about the important elements of the episode and to reflect on teaching strengths and deficits. Ownership in the rubric is inherent in the fact that all players participate in its construction. In a study conducted by Natriello and Dornbusch (1980/81), nearly one-half of the teachers did not know the evaluation criteria. Their principals, however, indicated that the teachers did know the criteria on which they were to be evaluated. Thus the researchers conclude, "Informing teachers of the criteria used to evaluate them is of prime importance if procedures for teacher evaluation are to have any impact on modifying and improving teacher performance. If teachers are unaware of the criteria and standards used to judge their performance, they are in no position to direct their energies along lines desired by the school organization" (p. 2).

Criteria selected for use in evaluating teachers should be supported by research and experience showing a relationship to desired learning outcomes. The evaluator has the task of determining whether teachers use effective teaching behaviors in appropriate situations. When evaluating instruction, five criteria are commonly used: knowledge of subject, preparation and planning, implementing and managing instruction, monitoring progress, and classroom environment. If, for instance, a rubric was to be developed for preparation and planning, criteria may be

- selects a variety of resources to support content
- prepares materials, equipment, and supplies in advance
- develops plans on daily and long-term basis
- develops instructional objectives to be met by students
- develops teaching procedures to match lesson objectives and student learning styles
- organizes content within time and learning constraints of the classroom
- designs a variety of assessment procedures to fit student learning needs
- prepares plans for substitute use, if needed

On a one to five scale, with five being the highest, the above criteria may be the five. The scale may be completed by adjusting the criteria to an average level for a three or to a low effectiveness scale using a one. Some teachers and evaluators may find it helpful to also create interim scales for a four and a two. An example of a rubric for preparation and planning is shown in Figure 10.1.

Another form of assessing teaching performance is through self-assessment. Stiggins and Bridgeford (1985) report that 53 percent of teachers desired more opportunity for self-evaluation. It is important for supervisors to know how teachers interpret their own teaching. Teacher self-evaluations are very useful for gathering data directly related to improvement. Carroll (1981) concludes that self-ratings are the most helpful when used to make comparisons with and interpretations of data collected from other evaluation sources such as principals, parents, or students.

There are three effective techniques for beneficial self-evaluation. One is the use of journals. A second is the use of personal rating instruments, which stimulates reflection, and a third is the viewing of video-

5   _____ selects a variety of resources to support content
         _____ prepares materials, equipment and supplies in advance
         _____ develops plans on a daily and long-term basis
         _____ develops instructional objectives to be met by students
         _____ develops teaching procedures to match lesson objectives and
               student learning styles
         _____ organizes content within time and learning constraints of the classroom
         _____ designs a variety of assessment procedures to fit the learning
               needs of students
         _____ prepares plans for substitute use, if needed

3   _____ selects limited resources to support content or resources lack variety
         _____ prepares most materials, equipment and supplies in advance
         _____ develops plans on a daily basis; long-term plans are sketchy
         _____ develops instructional objectives to be met by students; some may be
               inappropriate for developmental level or content
         _____ develops teaching procedures to match lesson objectives; variety to
               meet student learning styles is limited
         _____ organizes content within time and learning constraints of the classroom
         _____ designs assessment procedures to fit the learning needs of
               most students
         _____ prepares outline of plans for substitute use, if needed

1   _____ selects few resources to support content; with limited variety
         _____ is ill-prepared with materials, equipment and supplies
         _____ develops plans on a day-by-day basis
         _____ develops objectives with no clear instructional goal
         _____ develops teaching procedures with limited variation
         _____ organizes instruction with major timing difficulties
         _____ designs an assessment procedure without regard to student
               needs
         _____ prepares no plans for substitute use

Figure 10.1 Evaluation of Preparation and Planning Rubric.

taped lessons or microteaching episodes. Microteaching has been a part of teacher self-evaluation for the past three decades. As the name implies, microteaching is a simulated teaching experience of short duration involving the teaching of a lesson to a class of students. Orlich, Harder, Callahan, Kauchak, and Gibson (1994) provide the following rationale for the microteaching experience. Microteaching allows the teacher to

- practice a technique, strategy, or procedure
- reduce anxiety by practicing in a supportive environment
- test innovative approaches to a teaching concept
- develop specific delivery strategies such as questioning or closure
- experience self-evaluation and/or principal evaluation
- gain immediate feedback of experiences
- practice team teaching in a supportive environment

The procedure for teaching a microteaching lesson is simple. The teacher first decides the topic or process to teach, then prepares a plan of the lesson. The format of the lesson is pre-established. Specific performance objectives are outlined on the plan as well as materials needed, time constraints, and procedures for teaching the lesson. A conclusion and evaluation of the lesson's effectiveness in producing the desired objective ends the written lesson. The teacher then presents the lesson.

During the teaching experience, formative evaluations are taking place. The first is the assessment of the microteaching by the evaluator. Using a copy of the plan, written comments are made on the effectiveness of the plan to cover the objective, its portability, and the effectiveness of the implementation of the plan by the teacher. A collaboratively constructed rubric of essential criteria should serve as a guide (see Figure 10.2). Be positive regarding strategies and concepts effectively used. Note improvements needed in a constructive manner.

During the course of the microteaching, the lesson is videotaped. The goal of videotaping is to capture the interaction of the classroom. Once the initial novelty wears off, both students and teacher accept the presence of the equipment and the technician so the class proceeds with minimal disruptions. The videotaped lesson is reviewed first by the teacher who uses the pre-established rubric to critique the lesson. This review should be accomplished soon after the teaching event. From this self-evaluation, the teacher notes strengths and weaknesses in instructional design and implementation and sets goals for im-

Teacher's Name _____School _____

Grade/Subject _____   Principal _____

Date _____   Previously Targeted Goal(s)_____

5
- Uses eye contact
- Clarifies lesson (flow, accurate knowledge, clear directions)
- Articulates clearly, with good grammar
- Interacts with students positively
- Is organized and prepared
- Communicates at instructional level
- Uses appropriate facial expressions/body language
- Relates purpose; has closure
- Uses variety of attention-getting techniques in lesson
- Uses appropriate materials and high-level questioning
- Checks for understanding
- Uses mobility

3
- Makes eye contact occasionally
- Has some flaws in lesson delivery
- Uses poor grammar; articulation or clarity of voice is occasionally evident
- Interacts with students occasionally, or some interations negative
- Loses place in lesson; somewhat disorganized
- Communicates at instructional level most of lesson
- Generally has open and accepting facial expressions and body language
- Relates purpose and closure, though weak
- Uses attention-getting and varied strategies; sometimes ineffectively
- Uses appropriate materials and high-level questioning most of the time
- Randomly checks for understanding
- Is somewhat mobile in presentation

1
- Seldom uses eye contact or interacts with students
- Lacks clarity in lesson
- Lacks clarity in articulation; uses poor grammar
- Lacks organization; seems unprepared
- Is unsure of instructional level
- Uses unwelcoming facial expression and body language
- Is uncertain of purpose; closure is missing
- Lacks variety; lesson is not attention-getting
- Uses inappropriate materials; asks only low-level questions
- Provides no checks for understanding
- Lacks mobility

Comments:

Figure 10.2 Evaluation of Preparation and Planning – Microteaching Rubric.

provement. The tape and critique are reviewed at a later date simultaneously by the evaluator and teacher. The teacher explains the personal critique using the rubric, the video is viewed with comments made by either the teacher or evaluator, and the lesson plan with comments is given to the teacher. It is at this time that improvement goals are targeted. Figure 10.2 represents a rubric prepared collaboratively for a microteaching experience.

The frequency with which observations and evaluations are made is just as important as using the right instrument. Single annual visits are not conducive to improving instruction. Little and Bird (1984) observed that teachers claim a lack of faith in an evaluator who makes fewer than four visits per year. Closely related to the concept of frequency is the length or duration of the observation by the evaluator. A minimum of one-half hour is needed for the evaluator to determine whether specific instructional objectives have been met. Credibility of the evaluator must be maintained if the teacher is to reap the value of increased instructional effectiveness.

Yet another component necessary for growth in effective teaching is constructive feedback on the attainment of goals presented in a non-biased and timely fashion. Locke and Latham (1984) state that a sense of accomplishment and efficacy is a result of goal attainment, provided the goals are sufficiently challenging and success is meaningful. The use of rubrics provides teachers the necessary feedback. Specific criteria are discussed in terms of strengths or weaknesses. Instructional targets can then be set as improvement goals.

Just as collaborative rubrics should be generated to assess teachers, these same evaluation tools can be used to successfully evaluate principals. Joint discussion and development of administrative rubrics provide teachers with a means for assisting administrators in their roles. Teachers' opinions can be valid indicators of the effectiveness of administrators in facilitating improved instruction and as instructional leaders. Caution should be taken here, just as it is for teachers, that one evaluation instrument not be the sole source of decision making. Also, anonymity should be a rule in order to protect teachers from possible reprisal. Criteria that may be helpful in evaluating administrators include

- organizational and management skills for achieving instructional goals
- organizational skills for developing short- and long-term plans
- leadership skills for providing instructional direction
- leadership skills dealing with policy and legal issues
- supervisory skills for appropriate selection and assignment of staff
- professional skills that motivate and model appropriate behaviors
- management skills during times of conflict
- public relation skills for working with community members and parents

Harrison and Peterson (1988) state that principals most often cite public reaction as a measure of effectiveness. Teacher performance/morale, atmosphere of the school, and general quality of instruction are additional effective criteria stated. Figure 10.3 provides an example of a rubric used by teachers to evaluate principals.

Evaluations of educators should promote sound educational principles that include, but are not limited to, effective instruction. Criteria for evaluations should be selected for the purpose of instructional ef-

To be completed by faculty and staff. Please rate your principal according to performance observed over the past school year. Please respond to each characteristic by placing an X in the box having the numerical rating which best corresponds to your perceptions of leadership. Five is considered high while a one is considered to indicate performance at the lower end of a continuum. All responses will be kept confidential. Please do not put your name on this rubric.

	5	4	3	2	1
1. Has sufficient background in instructional strategies					
2. Provides assistance in helping improve instructional strategies					
3. Encourages personal and professional growth					
4. Is organized					
5. Manages with democratic style					
6. Helps to determine short-term goals for teachers and school					
7. Helps to determine long-term goals for teachers and school					
8. Knows policy issues required of a leader					
9. Knows legal issues required of a leader					
10. Is willing to seek and research answers					
11. Is up-to-date on current research in effective teaching					
12. Selects staff members that compliment the school culture					
13. Assigns staff members to appropriate roles considering time constraints, abilities and interests					
14. Handles situations appropriately and with tact					
15. Has the ability to motivate staff to get things done					
16. Is a role model for staff members and students					
17. Has good rapport with students					
18. Possesses adequate conflict management skills					
19. Supports the use of effective classroom management					
20. Handles difficult discipline problems with foresight					
21. Supports staff to the community and parents					
22. Has good writing skills					
23. Demonstrates good oral speaking skills					
24. Uses good listening skills					
25. Models confidentiality					
26. Keeps parents informed of school happenings					
27. Invites parents into the school community					
28. Invites community members to share in educating students					
29. Deals with problem situations in a timely manner					
30. Provides safe and healthy learning environment					

Figure 10.3 Principal Evaluation Rubric.

fectiveness. The collaborative effort and resulting dialogue that goes into developing the rubric used for evaluation is imperative. When all individuals are aware of and have input into the creation of criteria and descriptors, evaluation takes place from a common level, and buy-in occurs. It is through this process of meaningful and timely evaluation, using rubrics as a tool, that improvement in instructional effectiveness takes place.

REFERENCES

Adler, M. J. 1982. *The Paideia Proposal: An Educational Manifesto.* New York: Macmillan.

Boyer, E. L. 1983. *High School: A Report on Secondary Education in America.* New York: Harper & Row.

Carroll, G. J. 1981. "Faculty Self-Evaluation." In *Handbook of Teacher Evaluation,* J. Millman, ed., Beverly Hills, CA: Sage, p. 181.

Darling-Hammond, L., A. E. Wise and S. R. Pease. 1983. "Teacher Evaluation in the Organization Context: A Review of the Literature," *Review of Educational Research,* 53:285–328.

Duke, D. L. 1987. *School Leadership and Instructional Improvement.* New York: Random House.

Harrison, W. C. and K. D. Peterson. 1988, May. "Evaluation of Principals: The Process Can be Improved," *NASSP Bulletin,* 72:1–4.

Joint Committee on Standards for Educational Evaluation. 1988. *The Personnel Evaluation Standards: How to Assess Systems for Evaluating Educators.* Newbury Park, CA: Sage.

Little, J. W. and T. D. Bird. 1984. *Is There Instructional Leadership in High Schools? First Findings from a Study of Secondary School Administrators and Their Influence on Teachers' Professional Norms.* Paper presented at *The Annual Convention of the American Educational Research Association.*

Locke, E. A. and G. P. Latham. 1984. *Goal Setting: A Motivational Technique That Works!* Englewood Cliffs, NJ: Prentice-Hall.

National Commission on Excellence in Education. 1983. *A Nation at Risk: The Imperative for Educational Reform.* Washington, D.C.: U.S. Government Printing Office.

Natriello, G. and S. M. Dornbusch. 1980/81. "Pitfalls in the Evaluation of Teachers by Principals," *Administrator's Notebook,* 29:1–4.

Orlich, D. C., R. J. Harder, R. C. Callahan, D. P. Kauchak and H. W. Gibson. 1994. *Teaching Strategies: A Guide to Better Instruction* (4th ed.). Lexington, MA: D.C. Heath and Company.

Purkey, W. W. and J. M. Novak. 1984. *Inviting School Success* (2nd ed.). Belmont, CA: Wadsworth.

Smith, B. O., D. Peterson and T. Micceri. 1987. "Evaluation and Professional Improvement Aspects of the Florida Performance Measurement System," *Educational Leadership*, 44:16–19.

Stiggins, R. J. and N. J. Bridgeford. 1985, spring. "Performance Assessment for Teacher Development," *Educational Evaluation and Policy Analysis*, 7(1):95.

The Teacher Education Conference Board of New York. 1981. *The Effective Teacher*, Albany, NY: Author.

Wlodkowski, R. J. 1985. *Enhancing Adult Motivation to Learn*, San Francisco: Josey-Bass.

INDEX